# ENABLING
# EMPOWERMENT

**A Leadership Playbook for
Ending Micromanagement and
Empowering Decision-Makers**

**CHRIS SEIFERT**

PERFORMANCE
PUBLISHING

# CONTENTS

## THE 7-STEPS OF THE DECISION-MAKING FRAMEWORK

# Introduction

I HAVE ALWAYS thought of myself as a pretty good operations leader. In fact, I'm sure the people that know me well are smirking because I said "pretty good." Let's be honest, I have always thought I'm *darn good!* After all, I've been working in an operational capacity since I graduated from college and launched my first business offering restaurant cleaning services. With a modest investment of $800 and a vacuum cleaner, I embarked on a venture in the cleaning industry, servicing restaurants and nightclubs on a contract basis. This was an initiative initially conceived as a senior year project in college, which I then decided to actualize. And it worked.

The $800 investment and the vacuum cleaner paved the way for securing contracts, and I successfully expanded the business to the tune of more than $100,000 in annual revenue in the first year. In 1999, this was a huge deal and a significant achievement considering the initial investment and the value of money at the time. And the business was on the trajectory to double its sales in the subsequent year. During this period of rapid growth, I was fully immersed in the business, handling accounting, marketing, taxes, sales, and operations. I worked crazy hours to make this work. At this juncture, I only had a business partner and we employed three staff members.

However, everything changed when I watched a PBS special on submarines. It captivated me so much that, the following morning, after returning from a night shift, I informed my business partner of my intention to enlist in the Navy. He thought it was crazy for me to even think of that. Despite the disbelief, I was resolute in pursuing this new path and approached the recruiter, expressing my desire to serve as an officer aboard a submarine. They informed me I couldn't be an officer on a submarine because I hadn't taken calculus-based physics in college. However, he mentioned I could enlist, excel academically in Nuclear Power School, and potentially receive a waiver to become commissioned as a nuclear officer. Following his advice, I endured boot camp, completed the mechanical training at A-school, and tackled Nuclear Power School, coming out at the top of my class.

In fact, my academic performance at Nuclear Power School set a new precedent for GPA records among mechanics of that period. A few weeks before graduation, the Command Master Chief called me in, wondering why I was still there. Confused, I inquired what he meant. He pointed to my undergraduate achievement and current success in the program, probing why I hadn't entered as an officer to begin with. When I recounted my story and pointed to the waiver contingent upon my school performance, he informed me that I was being lied to. The Master Chief was direct, stating unequivocally that there was no waiver available for the path I had been pursuing. However, he offered me a new perspective by informing me about the existence of a non-nuclear officer role on a submarine — the supply corps officer. This alternative did not require a nuclear background, which piqued my interest since it gave me the opportunity to combine my operations expertise with the goal of getting onboard a nuclear submarine.

He recommended that I consult with the base's Supply Corps Officer for further insights. I engaged with the base Supply

Corps Officer, who shed light on the nature of the role. He detailed his responsibilities, which included managing the submarine's logistics, financial matters, as well as standing watch operating the vessel. His role was vital in running the "business" side of the submarine's operations, which was eye-opening. I reflected on how different my journey might have been had I known about this option earlier. Impressed by the scope of the supply corps officer's duties and realizing it aligned with what I sought, I decided this was the direction in which I wanted to take my naval career. The clarity and potential of this role resonated with me, prompting me to affirm my decision to transition into this new position within the Navy to land a commissioned position on the submarine instead of accepting for enlisted status.

My time in the Navy was transformative, equipping me with unparalleled technical engineering training and invaluable leadership experience. The rigorous curriculum of Nuclear Power School and my subsequent roles demanded precision, discipline, and a deep understanding of complex systems. This environment honed my ability to lead under pressure and manage highly technical operations with meticulous attention to detail. Additionally, I learned the critical importance of maintaining a rigorous, well-documented management system and fostering a culture of Operational Discipline. These lessons not only enhanced my professional capabilities but also ingrained in me the significance of structured processes and disciplined execution, which have been instrumental in my subsequent endeavors in the business world.

When I first left the Navy, my mindset was fixated on results. At that time, I thought success was quantifiable, that one must always focus on the numbers. To think otherwise would have taken a lot of convincing, given that just before my discharge I read *The Art of Execution* by Larry Bossidy and Ram Charan. This book, along with the teachings of Jack Welch, whose work I had also explored, underscored a philosophy of management that hinged on driving results and making decisions based on concrete numerical data. The narrow focus on outcomes, on results as the only indicator of success, was fundamentally flawed. The understanding of hindsight bias further complicated matters, given that past results might not always be the perfect metric for judging the efficacy of decisions or actions.

Acknowledging this, I learned leadership extends well beyond the realm of quantifiable results. True leadership involves the nuanced management of processes and systems—elements that are crucial, yet often overshadowed by the endgame of numbers. This realization required a shift from a results-only mindset to a more holistic approach to achieving objectives. When one strategy does not generate the desired results, there is no need to throw it out and start over. The focus just needs to shift to executing at a higher level when the next decision or strategy direction needs to be made.

I have come to appreciate that these concepts can be applied to transform our approach to leadership. My perspective on leadership has shifted to place a greater emphasis on the use of processes. It has become clear that the criterion for promotion should not just be good results. The right strategy is to promote those who apply processes to achieve their outcomes, because that is indicative of someone who can sustain success in the long run. I have witnessed several of my managers and executives achieve remarkable success in one context, but when they transitioned to a new environment, they struggled significantly. This pattern suggests that their initial success may not have been based on a robust or repeatable strategy; instead, it was likely a fortunate set of circumstances that could not easily be replicated. A well-defined process is critical because it provides a framework for consistent results, irrespective of varying conditions. Without a solid process in place, what appears to be success may be unreliable and unsustainable.

With these concepts firmly rooted in my mind, and further motivated by a "join the Navy, see the world" mantra, I felt ready to venture into the corporate sector, where I secured a position at Georgia Pacific as an Operations Excellence Specialist. In this role, I was tasked with multiple responsibilities: implementing maintenance reliability practices, contributing to operational strategy, and conducting analyses for sizable capital investment projects. It was also here that I was first introduced to Koch's Decision-Making Framework.

Georgia Pacific had been acquired by Koch Industries roughly a year prior to my arrival. During their first year at the helm, Koch Industries focused predominantly on integrating the Dixie division. Once this was under way, they turned their attention to the building products division, the sector where I was employed, marking the beginning of its integration into Koch's management framework. Koch Industries communicated to my supervisor, the General Manager of plywood, their intention to commit a substantial investment of approximately $50 million into the plywood segment. They sought his advice on which projects would yield the highest return on this investment.

However, the GM found himself at a loss, as he was unaccustomed to the level of analytical rigor Koch Industries expected. Traditionally, decision-making was based on straightforward profit and loss projections for individual plants, leading to a simple "yes" or "no" on potential initiatives. Koch Industries, on the other hand, required adherence to its specific Decision-Making Framework, which demanded more comprehensive economic analysis. The expectation was to engage in a thorough and robust evaluation to inform investment decisions, reflecting a shift toward a more sophisticated and strategic approach to managing business opportunities.

The GM recognized the complexity Koch Industries brought to the table with their decision-making requirements. Since I had a comprehensive understanding of business and strategy due to my background—an MBA and experience in operations—he saw it fit for me to take the lead and requested me to step in and determine the best way to invest this money. He expected me to not only to drive the investment decisions but also to master and then teach the Koch Decision-Making Framework to our team.

That's how I first engaged with the framework that would become a cornerstone of my professional expertise and the focal point of this book. It was an in-depth introduction that allowed me to learn and later teach a decision-making process refined through years of experience—a practice I've come to specialize in and share with others, molded by the legacy of that initial experience with Koch Industries. Thanks to this framework, I've served as the Plant Manager for three different manufacturing plants, each with 400+ employees and I was able to achieve significant improvements in productivity and reliability metrics at each one. Due to the success I experienced in those roles, my career progressed, culminating in the opportunity to serve as Vice President of Operations for a biomass fuel manufacturer where I led operations during a six-year period of rapid growth from four operating facilities to fourteen, and $350 million to $1.3 billion in revenue.

It's important to note that I refer to this as a framework and not a process for a reason. A process is rigid with clear parameters whereas a framework has a degree of flexibility. The amount of rigor and formality one applies to any given decision should be dependent on the situation at hand and not a one-size-fits-all approach, where those on the front lines have no autonomy or discretion. There is a big difference in the potential rigor one would apply to a decision, where the only downside outcome of one situation is that a particular machine is out of service for two hours, compared to another where the company stands to lose a five billion dollar investment if the wrong decision is made.

To best illustrate this in action, I'm brought back to a time when I was an incident commander in a plant where we had 40,000 tons of wood pellets stored in a dome that caught fire. We were a couple days into managing the incident and it was clear things were not getting better. The dome was getting hotter, the metal flexing to the point where we thought the door would blow off. I huddled together with the firefighters and engineers to brainstorm ideas on how we could respond rather than making a unilateral decision. Everything from spraying water on the door to burying the door was thrown in and we spent the next ten minutes evaluating the best courses of action.

To be clear, there were no bad ideas. This was an iterative process where we wanted to make sure everyone had a voice and was afforded the opportunity to explain their suggestion. From there, we were quickly able to rule out ideas. While water seemed like a logical winner, we had already been doing that to some degree for days and it was not getting better. Finally, we arrived back at what sounded like the most outlandish idea—burying the door. I had the engineer walk us through what that process would look like, and when he was done it no longer sounded crazy. We put the plan into action and it turned out to be successful. Burying the door prevented the dome from exploding—and it was all because we had this framework in place.

To help better share this Decision-Making Framework that got us through that near disaster and countless other challenging situations (DMF from this point forward for simplicity) with you, Chapters 4 through 10 will each breakdown one step in the chronological order one needs to follow to truly make it effective. At the end of each chapter, you will find a list of tools and templates you can download at www.enablingempowerment.com to assist you in your journey. After we explain each step and all it entails, we will look at some common decision traps that seek to derail your progress with examples as to how they may appear in your current organization. We will then extensively discuss how to either avoid falling victim to each of these traps or overcoming their grips when we find ourselves already falling victim to the biases they create. Just recognize as you read that there is no shame in admitting you have already been guilty of making decisions based on these false ways of thinking. We have all done it, and recognizing that fact is the first step in making better decisions.

# 1

# Why Empowering Your Team Is So Important

**THROUGHOUT MY CAREER,** across boardrooms and plant floors, I've heard a consistent theme: we need to empower our front-line employees. Most leaders I've interacted with recognize the empowerment of all employees as the pivotal element in achieving Operational Excellence and overall business success. A 2020 Harvard Business Review survey[1] backs this belief with a staggering 87% of organizations acknowledging that their potential success is tied to empowering front-line decision-makers. This wasn't a revelation.

However, here's the jaw-dropper. The same study reveals a mere seven percent of these organizations that acknowledge the need for empowerment actually arm their teams with the analytical tools and resources vital for autonomous decision-making. Is empowerment, then, just a buzzword? Or is there a systemic gap in its execution? In the numerous organizations I have ever worked for, or consulted with—with the exception of one—there was little evidence that the others took the time to implement such a process, as if it had really never been on their radar.

Many leaders treat empowerment like it's a magic wand—wave it, say the words, and *voilà*, teams will not only start making decisions but also consistently make the right ones. This perspective, though tempting, is far from reality. Drawing from my own journey managing large teams and consulting with multi-billion dollar companies, I've observed a pattern. Leaders genuinely wish to empower but often fall short on the execution. The intent is there, but the translation into actionable steps is amiss.

**Leaders genuinely wish to empower but often fall short on the execution.**

What most leaders miss is that, in order to empower their teams, they have to first enable them. At the risk of overgeneralizing, this requires two key elements. The first is a cultural shift. Leaders need to reorient themselves away from being decision-makers and into becoming mentors and coaches, guiding their teams through the decision-making process. The second is investing in upgrades to skills and resources. It is a sobering truth, but many front-line employees lack formal training in decision-making processes, often not by fault of their own but because of systemic education gaps.

> **What most leaders miss is that, in order to empower their teams, they have to first enable them.**

Empowering your employees, without first enabling them, feels a lot like entrapment from their vantage point. Imagine being a frontline employee suddenly bestowed with decision-making responsibilities but without being provided the necessary skills and tools. It's akin to being thrown into deep waters without swimming lessons or having no flight training and getting asked to fly a plane after the pilot becomes incapacitated. Despite official "empowerment" memos and speeches at town halls, the fear of making a misstep and the ensuing repercussions make many shy away and feel as though they have been "set up" to fail.

While there are a few companies and consultants striving to address this gap, I believe the majority are missing the point (including the *HBR* article referenced earlier). This is partly due to having a narrow focus on Data and Analysis. While data analytics is vital, decision-making is broader. We need a comprehensive approach that encompasses problem framing, identifying and evaluating alternatives, conducting economic analyses (at a level appropriate for a front-line employee), and effectively communicating the decision-making rationale.

A lack of reliability is another contributing factor. Many solutions do not cater to the unique challenges faced by real people, in real situations, in real time. This is especially true of operators and technicians in a manufacturing environment where most of my experience stems from, but the reduced efficiency resulting from it universally affects all industries. This is a systemic problem resulting from a focus on tools and processes instead of frameworks. Almost all decision-making courses available today focus on backward-looking evaluations instead of forward-looking predictions.

Some of these backward-looking tools include statistical analysis of how well a decision panned out, the use of AI in making or evaluating decisions, or rigid frameworks without much room for independent thought. For your people to make effective decisions, education and background do not matter nearly as much as developing the understanding of how to think things through. Most leaders do not want people to mindlessly come looking for answers without any potential suggestions at the ready; but for that to happen, they need a beginning-to-end process that is both scalable and applicable to real-life situations.

I recognized this early and tried to embody the principles of change when I began my career with Koch Industries. At the time, I supported approximately 12 to 15 facilities. I regularly made my rounds to each, imparting to the leadership teams the principles of the DMF and assisting them in the analysis of substantial capital ventures. I did not just want to tell them they had the power to make decisions on their own, I wanted to ensure they had all the tools needed to feel truly empowered.

Following a year and a half of these activities, I eagerly seized the chance to take full responsibility for managing one of the facilities. The plant was performing poorly, beset with numerous challenges. As I stepped in, my enthusiasm was palpable. A significant part of my past as a military officer persisted within me. It was important to me that my approach to leadership was empowering. My goal was to foster an environment where empowering individuals and teaching them decision-making skills was central to my methodology. The last thing I wanted was to be the autocratic leader who dictated every action.

However, I quickly realized that the facility I took over had been steeped in a culture of micromanagement, established by the previous plant manager. This realization struck me especially in my second week, when a shift supervisor approached me to help solve his problem. I was 30 years old, embarking on my first journey into civilian leadership at a company, and this seasoned machine operator was putting his faith in me rather than thinking it through on his own. But, instead of taking the easy way out, I had a particularly inspiring conversation with that shift leader and it was rewarding to observe his heightened engagement when we were done. Yet, it dawned on me quite swiftly that such an approach was unsustainable—enlightening 450 employees through one-on-one conversations was going to be challenging.

Realizing this, I began to focus on educating a broader audience. I committed myself to imparting the DMF not to every operator within the facility, but to many pivotal figures, particularly the supervisors of various departments and the shift leaders. The objective was clear: to transform the plant's operational mindset. We needed to move away from a dependency on the plant manager for solutions to every problem.

There is a simple reason why this autonomy was vital: I, myself, did not possess all the answers. Historically, Georgia Pacific had promoted plant managers from within their ranks. These individuals often rose from operator and supervisor roles, amassing knowledge over decades to eventually lead the plant. They were intimately familiar with the machinery and the business intricacies. This was not the case for me. Although I had been involved in the analysis of capital projects, my understanding paled in comparison to their expertise. Attempting to micromanage would have been futile, even if I had wished to. It was in this context that I originally began teaching the process. Eventually, the plant witnessed a remarkable transformation—marked improvements in both safety and operational performance. It was becoming clear to everyone that there was value in creating a culture of empowerment.

## Benefits of Empowerment

Empowering your teams by teaching them to be effective decision-makers is crucial. When done right, there is no doubt you're going to see improved decisions. People closest to the problem have better insight than you do—they always will. This is the foremost advantage of empowering them: once you've equipped them with the skills to make good decisions, the outcomes are enhanced because those individuals inherently have better access to information. They're closer to the customer, closer to the problem, and they possess a more detailed understanding which will always give them an edge. Sometimes the best decision is the quickest in the moment, minimizing downtime and losses, which cannot happen when frontline workers are wasting time looking for someone to help them.

When employees see their opinions are valued and the results of their decision-making efforts are having a positive impact on the company at large, they will be a more engaged workforce. When people believe a decision is truly theirs, they become more invested and determined to see it succeed than if they were simply following orders. This holds true even when they're merely making suggestions. For instance, if an employee recommends a course of action—let's say, "I think we should do X, Y, Z"—and you agree with it, they own that recommendation. They are accountable for it. They can't default to the excuse that they were only doing as instructed if things don't pan out. In a culture plagued by micromanagement, "I was just following orders" becomes an all-too-common refrain when faced with failure.

> In a culture plagued by micromanagement, "I was just following orders" becomes an all-too-common refrain when faced with failure.

By asking individuals to either make decisions or at least present recommendations, you immediately increase their engagement. They feel a stronger sense of ownership and responsibility for the results. Consequently, they are more committed to executing whatever is necessary to ensure the success of the decision. The buy-in process from making recommendations is also a great way to slowly and steadily build their confidence. There is a safety net of sorts in knowing that their leaders or managers would not blindly accept a harebrained suggestion if they did not see some merit in it. The more successful recommendations they make, the quicker they will be more comfortable executing on it without running it up the chain of command.

Work-life balance is another crucial benefit of empowering employees to make decisions on their own. Too often, work-life balance is used in the context of the hourly blue collar workers. When the labor force feels overwhelmed or overworked they are more likely to seek out positions at other companies with either higher pay or shorter shifts. But why do we ignore the amount of time leaders and managers put in to keep things running smoothly just because they do not punch a time clock? If you're the one responsible for all decisions, your personal life will suffer. You'll be bombarded with calls at all hours, leaving no room for personal time.

In the absence of delegating, work-life balance is non-existent, with constant inquiries and people seeking direction for every issue. Contrary to the popular belief we will cover in the next chapter, I truly believe most leaders do not want to be so enmeshed in the daily operations of their team that they fear taking a day off. One of the largest advantages of empowering others is the return of time. It allows managers to focus on their responsibilities, rather than being caught up in

> **One of the largest advantages of empowering others is the return of time.**

details suited for the plant level—details that, in many cases, should be addressed by the team itself. This empowers leadership to concentrate on strategic objectives that genuinely require their attention, fostering a more efficient and balance-driven work environment.

Better decisions develop a more engaged workforce, in turn allowing everyone, leadership included, a better quality of life. You don't need to be the captain of a nuclear submarine to realize the correlation among the three. But what you do need to do is take the first step in trusting your team enough to embark on this journey of empowerment. And to do that, you will likely need to change the way you think about leadership.

## What I Thought I Knew About Leadership

Not to brag, but I have been leading people for more of my life than I haven't been. With much of that training coming through the US Navy, I like to believe I know more than most about leading in general, but especially in high stakes environments. Early in my career I believed the formula for successful operations leadership involved a straightforward series of steps:

1.  Set a clear, measurable objective.
2.  Pick the best people and assign them accountability to achieve the objective.
3.  Empower those accountable to achieve it by providing them the necessary resources.
4.  Hold people accountable to the objective.

I'm not alone in my thinking on this. I got this formula early on in my career from leadership icons like Jack Welch and books like Execution: The Discipline of Getting Things Done[2]. But about a decade into my career, I was confronted with some data that had me seriously questioning this formula when my company sponsored an Operational Excellence Roundtable for Oil & Gas executives hosted by IQPC in Houston. This was an intimate setting with twenty or so VP-and-above executives from the oil and gas industry where they could discuss the most critical issues they were facing while leading their organizations to achieve Operational Excellence. One of the topics for discussion was the role of culture in achieving Operational Excellence.

To facilitate this culture discussion, we asked each of the executives to participate in a culture assessment using "yardstyck." Yardstyck is Wilson Perumal & Company's (WP&C) web-based culture assessment tool that allows a company to benchmark its culture against that of a High-Reliability Organization (HRO), which can be defined in various ways. But at its core, we are talking about organizations that consistently demonstrate superior performance in complex, high-risk environments over extended periods. One example of an HRO I am intimately familiar with is the U.S. Submarine Force, which is often revered as a paradigm of excellence. HROs are particularly relevant within the context of the Navy due to the inherently high-risk and complex nature of naval operations. The concept of HROs is exemplified by naval forces such as the U.S. Submarine Force, which operates under demanding circumstances where the margin for error is minimal.

An HRO is characterized by its heightened states of alertness and commitment to safety and precision, ensuring successful mission outcomes and the well-being of personnel. These organizations prioritize robust training, rigorous procedural compliance, and a culture of continuous improvement and learning. This focus on reliability and resilience is crucial in a naval context, where failure can have catastrophic consequences. The principles of HROs are integrated into many aspects of Navy operations, from the meticulous maintenance of submarines to the disciplined communication protocols among crew members. This adherence to HRO practices helps the Navy to consistently achieve its strategic objectives while safeguarding human lives and national security interests.

The integration of High-Reliability Organization (HRO) principles within the Navy revolves around five key pillars. These are designed to enhance safety, prevent errors, and ensure operational excellence, especially in high-stakes environments

- Preoccupation with Failure: Navy operations integrate this principle by paying close attention to the smallest signs of potential problems or errors. Regular drills, inspections, and debriefings are routine to catch and address any lapses before they escalate.
- Reluctance to Simplify: The Navy recognizes the complexity of its operations and, therefore, avoids oversimplifying situations, interpretations, and reports. This is crucial for understanding the nuanced risks associated with naval missions and for creating comprehensive strategies to manage them.
- Sensitivity to Operations: Continuous monitoring is a staple in naval operations. The Navy seeks to maintain real-time awareness of operations, ensuring that any issues can be quickly identified and responded to. This requires clear communication and a robust command and control structure.

- Commitment to Resilience: Training for resilience is integral in the Navy. Personnel are trained not only on how to perform their own duties with excellence but also to adapt and respond to unexpected challenges. The Navy prepares its members to cope with and recover from errors while maintaining operational capabilities.
- Deference to Expertise: While hierarchy is important in military organizations, Navy operations often defer decision-making to the person with the most relevant expertise, rather than strictly following rank. This ensures that informed decisions are made based on specialized knowledge, which is crucial in complex or emergent situations.

The integration of these HRO principles within the Navy involves not just the adoption of these mindsets, but also the development of processes and organizational structures that support them. It includes comprehensive training programs, advanced technology systems for monitoring and communication, and a culture that encourages reporting and transparency without fear of negative repercussions. Such integration is an ongoing process, requiring regular evaluation and adaptation to new situations and advancements. The Navy's commitment to HRO principles is a testament to their role in managing risk and ensuring mission success in one of the most demanding operational environments in the world.

Understanding high reliability organizations is not excessively complicated, and assessments of what constitutes an HRO can be somewhat subjective. While there is academic research on the topic, there is no formal governing body that grants an organization the official designation of being a "high reliability organization." The process of benchmarking against the metrics of an HRO has participants force rank different descriptors of organizational culture from those "most like" to "least like" their company's current culture. The process is then repeated, having them force rank the descriptors based on what they think the culture "should be like." WP&C has performed this process on HRO's like the U.S. Navy's submarine force, so we are able to show participants how their responses compare. Below is a screen capture from yardstyck so you can see what it looks like.

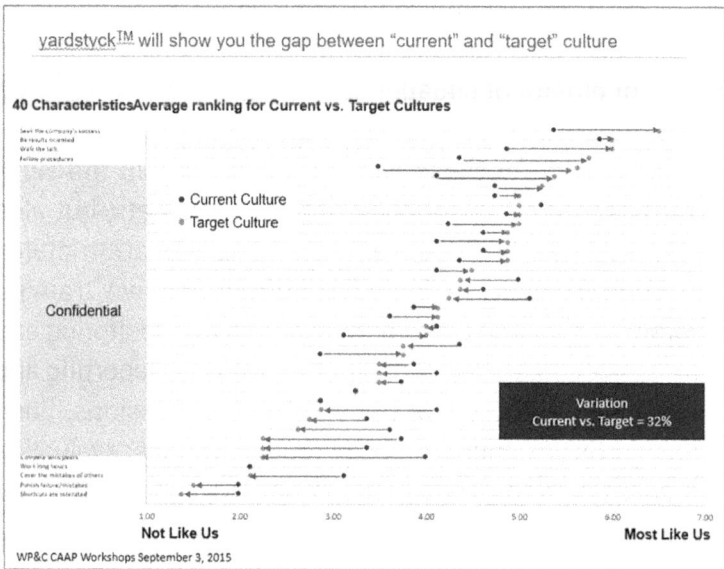

yardstyck™ will show you the gap between "current" and "target" culture

At first glance, I was very pleased with the data I saw from the executives. Largely, it confirmed a lot of my hypotheses. The data clearly showed that the executives believed they needed to have a culture like that of an HRO, but that there was a pretty substantial gap between where they are (the red circles) and where they want to be (the yellow circles). This was good news for someone who is in the business of helping them close that gap. But when looking more closely at the details, I saw something concerning—so much so that it even made me begin to question our model. The executives had ranked the statement "be results oriented" as third highest in their assessment of the current culture. What is more, they indicated they wanted even more of it by ranking it number one overall in the future state. Then I noticed "be results oriented" wasn't even in the top ten for the U.S. Navy Officers who had taken the assessment. In fact, it was number 24!!

This was shocking to me because I would have ranked "be results oriented" near the top, too. Remember my formula for operations leadership success? Clearly results are really important! So, what did this mean? Did it mean the Nuclear Navy is invalid as a benchmark for the private sector? After all, I was sure someone would point out that the submarine force doesn't have to worry about profit and loss or quarterly financial results. Maybe there was a lot to learn from the Nuclear Navy, but there were some things about its culture that just don't apply in the business world.

I began thinking our model might be flawed, but then realized the model was right and I was wrong. Having served on a U.S. Navy submarine, I knew results were important to my Commanding Officer and the rest of the leadership team. Maybe they just were not important in the same way. Maybe results weren't the end all and be all of management and leadership.

Then I had an epiphany and realized I heard this message before—results are not the most important thing. I heard it from another leader and organization that is the very definition of success in its industry; an industry which is hyper-competitive and extremely focused on results. In fact, in this industry, if an organization isn't performing at the highest level, the leader will almost certainly be fired within a year or two. As much as it pains me to say it, this leader and this organization have clearly been the best at what they do for almost two decades. I say it pains me because I am talking about Nick Saban[3] and the University of Alabama football team. (I'm a UGA grad – Go Dawgs!!)

For those who live under a rock, at the time of doing this study, Nick Saban and the Alabama Crimson Tide had won four of the last seven national championships. Clearly over that time span, Saban achieved the "results" that matter. But listen to what he has to say about what he and his leadership team focus on:

> *"Well, the process is really what you have to do day in and day out to be successful. We try to define the standard that we want everybody to sort of work toward, adhere to, and do it on a consistent basis. And the things that I talked about before, being responsible for your own self-determination, having a positive attitude, having great work ethic, having discipline to be able to execute on a consistent basis, whatever it is you're trying to do, those are the things that we try to focus on, and we don't try to focus as much on the outcomes as we do on being all that you can be."*

So, there you have it. It isn't a relentless focus on outcomes that leads to sustained superior performance. It is a focus on the process and the culture. Nick Saban said it. The officers in the U.S. Navy know it. And, I guess, now I know it too. But results are still important and I'm not saying that what I learned from all this is that I can ignore results. Nick Saban didn't say that, and neither did the Navy Officers. The Officers didn't rank "be results oriented" dead last. They ranked it in the middle. Nick Saban didn't say to ignore results. He said *"we don't try to focus as much"* on them.

**It isn't a relentless focus on outcomes that leads to sustained superior performance. It is a focus on the process and the culture.**

Results are clearly still important. They are how we measure the effectiveness of the "process," or what I refer to as the management system, and the culture. While we absolutely must step back periodically and use the results to evaluate the effectiveness of our management system and culture during periodic management reviews, we shouldn't manage the results on a day-to-day basis. What we should focus on daily is adherence to the management system and culture. Clearly this is a challenge in public companies where there is a relentless focus on quarterly reports to analysts and investors. But the data says that if you want to have sustained superior results, if you want to be a High-Reliability Organization, then you need to focus on the management system and culture.

1. Mattison, Ryan. "Nearly 90% of Organisations Say Success Depends on Empowering Frontline Employees to Make Decisions in the Moment, According to New Report." Businesswire. ThoughtSpot, May 5, 2020. https://www.businesswire.com/news/home/20200505005197/en/Nearly-90-of-Organisations-Say-Success-Depends-on-Empowering-Frontline-Employees-to-Make-Decisions-in-the-Moment-According-to-New-Report.

2. Bossidy, Larry, Ram Charan, and Charles Burck. 2009. Execution: The Discipline of Getting Things Done. 1st ed. Crown Currency. https://www.amazon.com/gp/product/B000Q9IR0A/ref=dp-kindle-redirect?ie=UTF8&btkr=1#detailBullets_feature_div.

3. Wikipedia. 2024. "Nick Saban." Wikimedia Foundation. Last modified July 24, 2024. https://en.wikipedia.org/wiki/Nick_Saban.

# 2

# Why Is it So Hard?

**NOW THAT WE** know empowering your team to make decisions without first enabling them to do so is like asking them to do a job with their hands tied, let's look at the main things you have to do to enable them to make decisions. The first is changing the culture of the organization. Leaders should act more like coaches, helping their teams think through choices instead of always making decisions. With this new culture in place, the next step is providing the right training and tools. Many of our team members haven't been trained on how to make good decisions, mainly because they never had the chance before.

Let's start with the first point and think about how leaders can drive the necessary cultural shift needed to foster an environment of empowerment. Intellectually, this isn't difficult. Leaders simply need to stop making decisions in isolation and engage frontline employees in the process. One very simple and practical piece of advice shared by retired US Navy Submarine Captain David Marquet in his book *Turn the Ship Around* (which I highly recommend) is to adopt the practice of asking for a recommendation, instead of giving direction. It's a beautifully simple practice I've used myself and encouraged the leaders who work for me to adopt as well. When leaders in the organization exercise the practice with discipline, the culture will change. Employees will learn that you want and expect them to be involved in the decision-making process.

However, given the countless survey results by experts that tell us leaders are not creating a culture of empowerment, we must conclude that leaders aren't adopting even this simple practice. Why is that?

We could take the pessimistic view, which would be that the majority of leaders and managers think their employees are incapable of making decisions, or that they just don't want to. Others might say it is because the leaders don't have a "servant leader" mindset nor do they believe they have an obligation to develop their teams. Still, others may argue that some leaders just think they are smarter than everyone else and want it done their way so everyone will know how smart they are.

While I will not argue that sometimes these situations could be the case, I just can't accept that these are the reasons the majority of initiatives to shift to a culture of empowerment fail. In my experience, most leaders truly believe they have an obligation to care for and improve the lives of the people they work for. They don't want to have to make every decision. And they are more than willing to invest their own time to coach and train their employees. Instead, I believe there are two fundamental reasons why this strategy fails.

Old habits are the first reason. For most leaders in an organization with a culture of micromanagement, telling their employees what to do is a reflex reaction. They don't even think about it. An employee comes to them and says, "The widget turner is broken; what do you want me to do?" The leader thinks about it and tells them what to do, without even realizing that they are perpetuating the norms of a micromanagement culture.

**For most leaders in an organization with a culture of micromanagement, telling their employees what to do is a reflex reaction.**

Sure, it is the easier thing to do at the moment, but what is it accomplishing for the long term goal of not having every employee come to management every time something out of the ritual and routine pops up?

Time is the other reason this strategy fails. In a micro-management culture, the one thing leaders definitely don't have is time. After all, they have to know everything about the business so they can make all the decisions. When an employee asks them, "What do you want me to do?"—it is much faster to just tell them. But as we just noted, this will only perpetuate the cycle of employees coming with more questions and ultimately taking more time from management than would have been necessary if they allotted the time up front to help the employee make the decision on their own.

> **In a micromanagement culture, the one thing leaders definitely don't have is time.**

While both issues are interrelated, the path forward to correcting the issues can be tackled separately. When it comes to habits, the best advice I can share is to learn to become very sensitive, almost allergic, to the phrases that indicate a culture of micromanagement. Two phrases I've learned to listen for, and have actually developed a physical response to hearing, are "What do you want me to do?" and "I just do what I'm told." Anytime I hear those phrases, I immediately stop and have a discussion with the employee about my desire for their participation in the decision.

Now, let me illustrate the challenge regarding time constraints with a personal example. Early in my tenure as a Plant Manager at my first plant, I had a Shift Leader come up to me and tell me about a problem with one of the plywood presses he worked on. Apparently, one of the forty openings on the press had failed. That meant we would be losing 2.5% of the capacity of that press until it was repaired. He then asked me, "What do you want me to do?"

I dutifully replied, "I'd like you to make a recommendation."

It was clear from the look on his face he had never been asked this before. He was so uncomfortable that he did everything he could to avoid answering the question, trying to get me to just tell him. Now, in this case, it helped that I was new to the plant and didn't know the answer off the top of my head either, but I was also determined to show him that I wanted him to participate in the decision-making process. So we spent the next thirty-plus minutes discussing the alternatives (shut it down now and fix it on an unplanned basis, run until the next outage, fix it tomorrow on a planned basis). We then walked through the financial implications of each of the alternatives. At the end of our discussion, there was one alternative that the math said was clearly the right one.

The thing about it was, he knew the information and he knew how to do the math; he just didn't have the practice of using or explaining a decision-making process. While I was totally energized by the discussion, as was the shift leader, it quickly dawned on me that I had a huge problem. There were more than 400 employees in that plant, and even if I recruited all the other managers (there were only about a dozen), it would take us forever to have that exact same conversation and go through that exercise with each employee. I wouldn't have time to do anything else.

I believe this is the fundamental reason that so many initiatives to empower frontline employees fail. It's not because the leaders don't want to empower their teams, or because they believe they are incapable of ever making good decisions; rather, it is because after a few attempts like the one I described, they have to give up and go back to being directive, or nothing will get done. But the challenge of time constraints should in no way absolve leaders from making the behavior shift needed to drive the cultural change, but it does mean we have to take a more strategic approach to teaching employees how to make and communicate decisions.

This finally brings us to the second issue surrounding the right tools and training, which is an all-too-common oversight. While there is a keen intent to enhance the cultural framework to empower teams, there is often a lack of attention to upgrading training and providing the right tools. This oversight is precisely what makes the process seem so arduous. More often than not, we tend to overlook the important part which entails providing the training and tools required for this empowerment. Addressing this, importantly, could help organizations escape the vicious cycle of the micromanagement doom loop.

The pattern is all too familiar. Leaders proclaim their desire to empower their teams, broadcasting messages like, "I want to empower you," or "I expect you to engage in decision-making," and "I encourage you to make recommendations." Yet, the team often lacks the necessary know-how for such tasks. Without the right proficiency, team members falter, crafting subpar recommendations. This can quickly disillusion leaders, who may react by reverting to a directive style, telling their staff precisely what to do. Consequently, this cycle of attempted empowerment followed by retreat into micromanagement recurs, trapping both the leader and their teams in a repetitive loop that undermines true empowerment.

We will address the cultural change in the last chapter of the book, but the question arises—how does one effectively implement change? The logical next step is to furnish the appropriate training and tools. Upon reflection, it is clear that providing training and tools should actually precede the onset of driving significant cultural shifts. Otherwise, the efforts may not be as successful as intended. Before worrying about culture shifts, we should concentrate on delineating the exact training that needs to be provided and the processes that should be established. Once that training is underway and people start to gain competence—becoming more capable of making informed decisions—that is the moment to initiate a shift in approach. At this point, we can step back and guide rather than dictate, allowing individuals to apply their new skills and knowledge independently.

> **Before worrying about culture shifts, we should concentrate on delineating the exact training that needs to be provided and the processes that should be established.**

By applying this framework, in the future a working dynamic will evolve to become more interactive and advisory. The employees will be encouraged to present recommendations to their leader, which will foster a more participatory environment. It is essential, though, that we set the stage for this approach by ensuring there is a solid foundation of skill development first. We need to prioritize building these capabilities before we shift into a mode where the employees are advising rather than just executing tasks.

## Do Leaders Really Want to Micromanage?

There are many misconceptions as to why some leaders tend to be micromanagers. Best-selling authors and organizational culture gurus will tell you it is because the person is a control freak, a narcissist, and every other term under the sun. But what these so-called experts will not tell you is that most of them have never managed a team of people themselves. They do not know the first thing about the complexities involved with people leadership, especially in complex industries where fast and accurate decision-making skills are critical to success. They can't speak to the constraints put on their time by the sheer volume of questions, problems, and situations they are asked to step into on a daily basis.

## So why then do leaders become micromanagers?

Usually, it is because they have no choice. There is just not enough time in the day to stop each time a direct report comes to them with an issue and coach them through a decision-making process. All the time they spend trying to do that is directly taking away not only from their own work, but also from all the other employees who are waiting for assistance with the issues they are facing. This conundrum, or doom loop, which we will explore shortly, reminds me of an experience I had while in the Navy.

During preparation for our intense sixth-week Room Locker and Personnel (RLP) Inspection at Officer Candidate School (OCS), an event that could grant us our first taste of liberty, our class found ourselves in an unexpected scenario. Gunnery Sergeant Jones, our Class Drill Instructor from the

United States Marine Corps, had us stand at attention and instructed us to "take notes." This was unusual, to say the least, considering the subject matter: ironing pants.

Gunny Jones proceeded to delve into the intricacies of pants-ironing with meticulous detail, an exercise that seemed absurd given the fact that we had the background and qualifications necessary to make it into OCS to begin with. As I stood there with my arm trembling from holding my notepad out straight in front of me (the proscribed "note-taking" posture), I couldn't help but wonder, *Does he think I'm stupid? I've been ironing my pants since Junior High, and I have a college degree!*

After what felt like an eternity, Gunny Jones finally allowed us to lower our arms and shifted the focus to our thoughts. "Some of you are wondering why I'm teaching you to use an iron," he said. "You have college degrees, you've been ironing pants for years, and you know how to use an iron. Does that mean I think you're stupid?" At that moment, I was convinced he could read my mind.

Gunny Jones continued, "I know you have a college degree, and you don't have to iron your pants exactly like this. If you think you've got a better way, fine. You can iron your pants however you want. I'm just saying that tomorrow when they come to inspect your pants, they better look like this. And if they don't, I'm going to ask you why you didn't iron your pants the way I showed you."

In that enlightening moment, I realized the lesson wasn't about ironing pants but about leadership and empowerment. What Gunny Jones taught me was that, as a leader, he had multiple responsibilities to those in his charge. The first was to demonstrate the expected outcome, setting the standard for what everyone's results should look like after a process is complete. He did not want half our class to have pants look one way while the other half was different. That might not seem like such a big deal with uniforms, but imagine what happens if the same is allowed to happen with a more complex process and high stakes outcome, like building a submarine or charting a course in enemy waters.

Gunny Jones also knew he had to ensure we had the necessary knowledge and skills needed to achieve the outcome he was demonstrating. While the lesson he was teaching was basic by all counts, he made it a point of ensuring we had the essential skills. Leaders could even take this a step further by confirming their direct reports also have the necessary tools to achieve the outcome. Had there been no irons in our room locker, it would have been impossible to iron the pants at all, let alone as instructed. So, it doesn't matter how well you explain the pallet-stacking strategy to a warehouse foreman if they were never taught how to operate the forklift!

The final take away from Gunny Jones was in his desire to not just give blanket authority to iron our pants however we wanted, but to let us know we would be held accountable for meeting his expectations. He demonstrated a proven way to get the end result he wanted, but he was not planning on standing over our shoulders as we performed the task. Micromanagement becomes unnecessary when your people know what the expectation is, have at least one proven way of getting there, and understand that no excuses will be accepted if they try to do something a different way without achieving the desired result.

Leadership, as I learned that day, hinges on these three components. If any one of them is missing, true empowerment is compromised:

1. Without demonstrating the expected outcome, team members may lack a clear understanding of the goal.
2. Focusing solely on the "how" and not the "outcome" leads to micromanagement and stifles creativity.
3. Failing to hold team members accountable for the outcome can result in missed opportunities and disappointment for the entire team.

On a side note, I'm still not sure there was a lesson to be learned from having to hold our arms straight out to "take notes" the whole time. Part of me suspects that was for his own amusement. But in all seriousness, Gunny Jones may have been teaching us to iron our pants, but the real lesson was in leadership and empowerment. As leaders, our responsibility is not just to set the path but also to equip our team with the tools and freedom to excel, all while holding them accountable for reaching the destination. This lesson from OCS has stayed with me throughout my career, reminding me of the importance of empowering and trusting your team for success.

Leaders who fail to follow these key steps are creating a self-fulfilling prophecy where they will be forced to micromanage and they have no one to blame but themselves. To this day, I embody the spirit of Gunny Jones' message in my daily management duties. One such instance occurred at a wood pellet manufacturing plant I was responsible for as the VP of Operations for the company. They were struggling to meet their production targets because of a bottleneck in their process that we traced back to the step where the raw wood needed to dry before it could be broken down further to reach its end state of pellets.

There was a large unit—a rotary drum dryer, probably close to a hundred feet long by twenty feet in diameter—that was responsible for drying the wood chips. The dryers were the least capable machines within the plant's ecosystem. Whatever output the dryers could achieve dictated the volume of wood chips the rest of the plant could process into pellets. To get a better understanding of the problem, I began running the dryer myself and my team witnessed me at the control panel for this machine countless times as I consistently hit our target with an inlet temperature of 1,000 degrees. It should not have been a revelation that hotter air dries more wood, which is why my results at 1,000 degrees far surpassed what they were doing at 850 degrees.

They were resistant and kept arguing with me about the process despite the proven success I was experiencing compared to their prior failures. Finally, I relayed the iron pants story to them, emphasizing that this was their plant and that at the end of the day, they were accountable for this plant's performance, not me. So, the responsibility to operate the dryer falls on you. I have shown you how to run it efficiently, and I have demonstrated the method to achieve the target wood production. I did it, and you watched me reach a thousand degrees in temperature. If you believe there is a better way to do it, that is perfectly acceptable—try it. However, if you fail to meet the target, I will question why you did not use the thousand-degree temperature setting, as I have recommended.

In telling my team the iron-your-pants story, my aim was to help them understand the core principle. Just as with the story, I have laid out the target for you. I have shown you a method that works. If you think you have a better method, that is great—go ahead and give it a shot. But if it falls short of the target, I expect no excuses. You have witnessed the process's effectiveness because I just demonstrated it. So why can't you replicate it? The plant manager acknowledged the point, saying, "I get it. I have to iron my pants." And with that we both knew we were on the same page and the only way we were going to revisit the conversation was if my method of drying at 1,000 degrees ceased working or if they innovated a way to improve the process at a different temperature.

When it comes to fostering a culture that enables our people to thrive, we can draw lessons from this story. Once the team acknowledges that you have given them the necessary tools and training, the leader must clarify that the provision of these tools and training does not dictate the exact methods they must employ. Leadership is not about dictating every step you take; it is about collaboration and trust. If you come up with a superior method or have a unique insight, I'm all for it—go ahead and implement it. The essential part is that we're on the same page now. I've done my part in providing you with the resources you need to succeed.

Once you confirm you have everything required, the responsibility shifts to you. You are not just responsible for carrying out tasks but also for delivering the anticipated results and outcomes. Feel free to forge your own path and make decisions that you believe will lead to success.

However, remember that with this freedom also comes a level of accountability. It's that ownership of the results that truly defines our collective success and your personal growth.

One of the challenges leaders often face is the discomfort associated with relinquishing decision-making authority or accountability. They may think, "If I allow my team to try different approaches, can I still hold them responsible for the outcome?" And the answer is yes. After demonstrating the standard method, they remain accountable for the results. Leaders should empower their team members to innovate while ensuring accountability is maintained.

**One of the challenges leaders often face is the discomfort associated with relinquishing decision-making authority or accountability.**

Of course, if an approach is evidently hazardous or likely to fail—for instance, an unsafe way to iron pants—it's the leader's responsibility to intervene and prevent that method from being attempted. Indeed, there are clear boundaries. For instance, you wouldn't iron your pants while wearing them. Similarly, if someone proposed ironing their pants while on their body, I would firmly say no. That approach is out of the question—it's unsafe and not endorsed by any reasonable standard. At that juncture, I would insist on adherence to the proven methods I've already laid out because deviating in such a manner is not just unproductive but potentially harmful. Moreover, suggesting something so fundamentally flawed might prompt a serious discussion about their judgment and future in their position.

## The Micromanagement Doom Loop

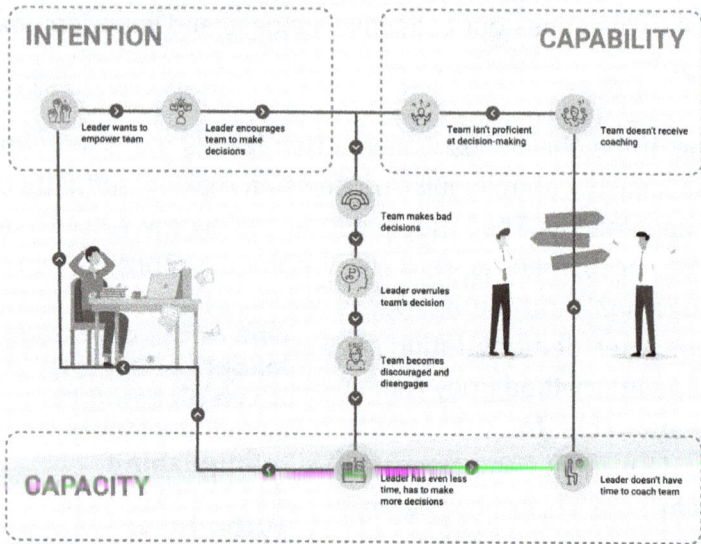

**INTENTION**

- Leader wants to empower team
- Leader encourages team to make decisions

**CAPABILITY**

- Team isn't proficient at decision-making
- Team doesn't receive coaching

- Team makes bad decisions
- Leader overrules team's decision
- Team becomes discouraged and disengages

**CAPACITY**

- Leader has even less time, has to make more decisions
- Leader doesn't have time to coach team

The micromanagement doom loop is the equivalent of a vicious cycle or death spiral when it comes to the health of an organization. No leader at any level wants to fail, or see their people fail (at least I hope not), yet they continue doing the same things day after day and expecting a different, or better, result the next time. We've probably all heard this referred to as the definition of insanity but, in the moment, most of us think we are doing the right thing. Why the disconnect?

Leaders want to empower their teams to make recommendations or decisions. No one wants to be needed to answer every mundane question or routine problem as they arise. It would be impossible to get anything else done. When the leader is doing the job of the frontline employee, there is no need to pay the two salaries—just put the leader in charge of the process and problem solved! The problem is that, even though leaders want their employees to be empowered and more self-sufficient, these people are not proficient at making good decisions. Therefore, the recommendations they make are not good.

The leader becomes overwhelmed with making all the decisions to avoid having whatever the situation is getting out of control, and in the process they forfeit the time they could have been using to provide coaching and mentorship on the decision-making process. This lack of coaching and support causes the team to become discouraged and disengaged. When a team becomes discouraged and disengaged, they are more likely to increase their dependance on the leader, which in turn makes the leader even busier than they already were. Eventually, with no time left to do their own job, the leader starts delegating more decisions to the team. But this is the same team that was not enabled with the decision-making skills to handle the responsibilities they have been empowered with, and the doom loop repeats itself.

My favorite way to describe a real life example of how many leaders find this doom loop manifesting in their organizations is being in the difficult position of watching someone drowning in a lake. If you have ever had the unfortunate experience of watching someone nearly drown, you probably know what I am describing. Arms flailing wildly in the air in attempts at both staying afloat and signaling for help; head bobbing above and below the water line; frantic screams and cries for help muffled by the gurgling water rushing into their lungs. Heck of a dramatic scene, right?

Now, let's say you are on the shore watching this unfold. What do you think most people would do in that situation: take the time to try walking them through the mechanics of swimming back to shore or staying afloat, or jump in to save them? I like to believe any who could swim would opt for the second option. This is the very situation leaders find themselves in on a daily basis when they watch their teams execute poorly on decision-making processes. The difference is, in the lake example, only the person in the water is at risk of drowning. In an operational environment, poor decision-making can be so bad that everyone in the building is getting put at risk if the leader does not step in and make the "executive call."

Not every situation is going to be quite as dire as watching someone potentially drown or suffer other grievous bodily harm, and often they can be used as learning situations. I recall a particular afternoon following a church service where we had a small social gathering at a nearby park. My daughter, quite young at the time, was eagerly scaling the monkey bars. Observing this, a friend of mine expressed concern, approaching me with a question, "Hey, aren't you worried she might take a tumble and injure herself?'

I paused, watching her navigate the bars with determination and then responded half-jokingly, "Well, she probably won't die, right?" Their expression was one of disbelief, prompting me to elaborate, "What I mean is, while she may fall, it's not likely to be life-threatening." The idea was to convey a level of acceptable risk and the importance of allowing her the autonomy to navigate obstacles while understanding the potential consequences. There was a chance she could sustain an injury, and if that happened, it would be a learning moment. Chances are, once someone realizes there is pain, or other negative consequences associated with an action, they will think more carefully about it in the future.

Much like all leaders will experience with their employees, this concept of experiential learning wasn't new in my relationship with my daughter. I distinctly recall an incident from her early years when she had a habit of pulling out the drawer at the bottom of the old-style stoves, where the pots were stored, to use it as a step and reach the stove top. We tirelessly cautioned her about the dangers, reiterating, "Don't touch the stove; it's hot."

On an unrelated front, one day she wandered into the laundry room and, out of curiosity, touched the iron, resulting in a burn on her hand. And so I asked her, "Annalee, what happened? You know the iron is hot." While she cried, I comforted her, addressing the pain from the burn. The very next day, Annalee was back to her usual antics, pulling out that drawer to reach the stove. I cautioned her, "Annalee, remember not to touch the stove; it's hot."

She paused, looked at me, and asked, "Like the iron, Daddy?"

I replied, "Exactly like the iron."

That was the last time I ever had to warn her about the stove. And through this, I learned an important lesson—sometimes it's more effective to let people experience a small setback. They tend to learn much quicker from their own mistakes than from us constantly trying to shield them from failure. Of course, I draw the line when it comes to serious harm; if touching something poses a permanent danger, I wouldn't allow it. But in certain cases, a minor incident can be a profound teacher.

## Why Aren't People Good at Making Business Decisions?

There is one simple answer to this question. We are not taught how to make decisions. Sure, we all learn, albeit informally, how to make a choice between two options. But no one ever sits us down to discuss what made us make one choice instead of another. Most of the decisions we make are based on intuition or from learned experiences. If you think I am joking, ask yourself how many educational institutions you know of that teach formal decision-making classes as part of their curriculum. High schools sure don't. Bachelor's Degree programs don't. Heck, I have an MBA, which one might think would be the place to learn this, and never once in that program were we taught how to make decisions.

The problem is that these institutions and programs do not even realize they are missing such a key skill in the business world. They may teach elements of decision-making, like how to leverage tools to conduct analysis or useful metrics to look back and evaluate the impact of a decision that has already been made. But no one goes through the process of decision-making from start to finish with a specific framework that works in any situation.

The second piece of the puzzle is what I like to call Decision Traps, which we will be covering at length in this book. These traps come in many forms and can have a range of impact on the decisions people in your organization make, but they contribute to flawed thinking in one way or another. Throughout my career I have been frequently presented with requests from engineers who wanted millions of dollars in capital investments into various programs or initiatives. It quickly became apparent to me that many, if not all, of these engineers had no idea how to assess the impact of the investment dollars they were seeking.

Almost all project spreadsheets required an estimate of the net present value (NPV), and there would be monetary sums filled out in those columns. But when I would ask an engineer to walk me through how they arrived at that number, to show me the calculations, I was met with blank stares more often than not. They also lacked the comprehension of concepts such as opportunity cost and how to conduct marginal analysis. What I consider to be fundamental economic skills necessary for an effective decision-making process are missing more often than not.

## Decision Traps

Before we dive into the DMF that I have used and taught to my teams and that you can deploy across your organization, I want to delve a little deeper into what decision traps are, how they lead to bad decisions, and how adopting a DMF can help mitigate their impacts.

In the 1970s, psychologists Amos Tversky and Daniel Kahneman wrote several groundbreaking papers credited with founding the modern-day discipline of behavioral economics, for which Kahneman was awarded the Nobel Prize for Economics in 2002. Many popular books like *Freakonomics*[4] and *Nudge*[5] have their bases in the concepts introduced by Tversky and Kahneman. In one of their most famous papers, Judgment under uncertainty: Heuristics and biases,[6] they describe the problem of cognitive bias in decision-making as follows:

> "People rely on a limited number of heuristic principles, which reduce the complex tasks of assessing probabilities and predicting values to simpler judgmental operations. These heuristics are generally quite useful, but sometimes they lead to severe and systematic errors."

To say that in simpler terms, we are faced with making millions, if not billions, of decisions daily. What to wear, what to eat, when to leave, who to sit next to, etc. To prevent our brains from exploding, our minds create "mental shortcuts" that make decision-making easier. While these mental shortcuts are incredibly helpful (we would be paralyzed with indecision if we didn't use them) and generally very efficient, they sometimes lead to catastrophic errors. For instance, consider the following example:

> A neighbor has described an individual as follows: "Steve is very shy and withdrawn, invariably helpful but with little interest in people or in the world of reality. A meek and tidy soul, he has a need for order and structure and a passion for detail." Is Steve more likely to be a librarian or a farmer?

If you are like most people, your initial intuition is that Steve is more likely to be a librarian. Would you reconsider your answer if I told you there are roughly 200+ farms for every library in the U.S.? Which facts are more relevant in making your estimate? The fact that there are 200 times more farms than libraries, or that Steve is described as "a meek and tidy soul"? Clearly, it should be the ratio of farms to libraries, but did you even think about that before being provided the data?

So why isn't it obvious to so many of us to ask about the ratio of farms to libraries? The answer is that our brains just aren't wired that way. Most of us aren't very good at mental math, and even if we were mental gymnasts, we wouldn't have time to do statistical calculations for every decision we make. So, our brains have created simple rules to make decisions faster.

**Our brains have created simple rules to make decisions faster.**

In this case, we likely have a "stereotypical" image of a librarian in our mind (whether it is accurate or not is another discussion). Since the description of Steve fits our stereotypical image, we defaulted to saying Steve is more likely to be a librarian.

While these mental models are essential and, in most cases, work really well, they can lead to catastrophic results in others. For instance, when evaluating an investment decision that appears to be similar to other investments we remember as working out well, we may not always ask for or consider all the data that is truly required to evaluate whether or not it is a good idea. That investment can be anything from purchasing the same type of equipment you have used in the past without realizing the manufacturer has moved their plant overseas and quality has been reduced, to bringing in the same outside QA firm you always use to ensure operational efficiency without realizing the senior leadership team has changed.

As we get into the specific steps of my DMF, there will be very specific traps that could easily trip someone up and prevent them from achieving an effective outcome. But to be able to understand those decision traps, it is important to understand some of the ways the human brain works. I promise, this is not going to become a science or psychology lesson, but the basic decision-making functions in the brain are critical. To explain this, I am going to continue leveraging and referencing the work of renowned psychologist Daniel Kahneman.

Kahneman breaks down the brain's decision-making functions into two systems, aptly referred to as System 1 and System 2. This is important because, as we have already established, we are all asked to make millions of decisions every day. If you had to think critically about each of these decisions, you would quickly become overwhelmed and nothing would get done. Your brain uses these two systems to distinguish between what can be resolved quickly with minimal thought and what will require more concentrated focus.

| Characteristics of System 1 | Characteristics of System 2 |
| --- | --- |
| • Fast, snap judgments<br>• Unconscious reasoning<br>• Judgments based on intuition<br>• Correlation and association<br>• Large capacity<br>• Effortlessly and automatically<br>• Influenced by experiences, emotions, and memories | • Slow, deliberate decisions<br>• Conscious reasoning<br>• Judgments based on examination<br>• Cause and effect<br>• Small capacity<br>• Requires effort and control<br>• Influenced by facts, logic, and evidence |

$$17 \times 24 =$$

Looking at the characteristics of System 1 above, it might become clear why you are able to immediately arrive at the determination that the woman on the left side is angry. It does not take much time or effort to come to the conclusion that this woman is angry. If you saw her coming at you in the street, the overwhelming reaction would be to get defensive because System 1 does not need much preparation to jump to that conclusion. But when we look at the math problem on the right side, the mind moves slower. System 2 does not allow you to jump to conclusions because the calculation is too complex to solve without taking the time to evaluate. That could involve looking for a calculator, pencil and paper, or thinking back to grammar school math classes on how and when to carry the excess digit.

The fact that our brains are designed in this way is actually good for us in the long run and one of the only reasons we are able to get anything done on any given day. Imagine if your brain needed to focus intently on everything you encountered on the drive to work: the squirrel in the tree, the woman walking into the coffee shop down the block, the clouds shifting overhead—okay, you get the point. If those various situations were not subconsciously processed by System 1, we would never make it out of the parking lot. And if you did, you would be mentally exhausted from all the effort required before ever making it to your destination.

Keeping System 1 and System 2 in mind, let's look at the graphic below:

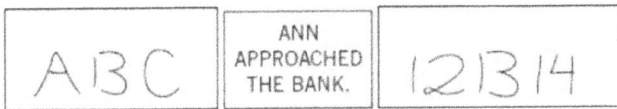

Looking at the box on the left, it seems pretty clear that the pattern is A, B, C. Ignore the middlebox and go to the right box where the pattern is a pretty obvious 12, 13, 14. Or are they? Take a closer look and you might notice that the B and 13 are written the same way. But your brain doesn't process the image like that because System 1 is trying to make a decision as fast as possible so that you can protect System 2 and preserve brain power. It is also important to note here that System 2 is predisposed to accept the quick answers System 1 comes up with, unless it is actively tasked with verifying or disproving the result.

Now ask yourself about the statement in the center box. Depending where you are at this very point in time, your perception of what is happening could be very different. If you are in your office in a busy city center, you probably envision a woman in a business suit approaching a financial institution. However, if you are reading this on the beach, you might see a woman in a bathing suit approaching the shore, or bank. Our current reality is very good at tricking System 1 into believing whatever is the easiest and fastest decision. But there's more!

Which of the three figures above is the tallest? System 1 wants to jump to the conclusion that it is clearly the figure to the far right. System 1 has learned over time that converging lines indicate distance, which would have to mean that the figure on the right is further away from the others and therefore must be taller than the others. But if you were to take a ruler and measure each of the figures, it would become obvious that they are all the exact same size. Chances are you just read that and still can't believe it to be true unless you activate System 2 and go find a ruler to confirm it to be the truth.

Why did we just spend so much time learning about the psychology of decision-making? Because the very systems that are in place to protect us from inaction, fatigue, and overcomplications are also the ones that can get us into trouble when we have to make choices. As we will learn in each of the steps of my DMF, there are very specific traps that will lure you into a false sense of security. The right answer may seem apparent in the moment, only to find out afterward you were acting without having all the facts. To be effective at avoiding these traps, we need to find the right balance between System 1 and System 2.

> **The very systems that are in place to protect us from inaction, fatigue, and overcomplications are also the ones that can get us into trouble when we have to make choices.**

One of the things putting System 1 and System 2 at odds in the decision-making process is the concept of "what you see is all there is," which opens the door for almost all the decision traps we are going to cover during the steps of the DMF. This concept tells the brain that the only factors worth considering are the ones we can plainly see, which System 1 likes because it can then make a quick determination without having to activate System 2. It allows the brain to overlook the numerous other options or consequences that could be just beneath the surface.

This occurs because System 1 makes a simplifying assumption. It effectively reasons, "I must make a decision based on the information immediately in front of me." This assumption often guides our judgment, explaining why one might overlook essential statistical context and how this inclination contributes to decision-making errors. Certainly, the notion of "what you see is all there is" warrants deeper exploration as it pertains to the identification of common decision-making traps, which will also be covered in much greater detail as we go along.

The value of having a defined, common DMF is that, if structured properly, it can help us identify our blind spots and minimize the likelihood of getting caught in a decision trap. It forces us to slow down and ask specific questions that help surface the information we haven't thought of. Helping individuals to look at every situation in a bubble and evaluate them on their own merit at that very moment in time breaks the cycle of assuming that what worked well in the past will automatically do so again and that prior poor outcomes will also continue yielding poor results.

> **The value of having a defined, common DMF is that, if structured properly, it can help us identify our blind spots and minimize the likelihood of getting caught in a decision trap.**

4. Levitt, Steven D., and Stephen J. Dubner. "Freakonomics." Freakonomics. Accessed March 31, 2024. https://freakonomics.com/books/.

5. Thaler, Richard H., and Cass R. Sunstein. 2009. Nudge: Improving Decisions About Health, Wealth, and Happiness. 2nd ed. Penguin Books. https://www.amazon.com/Nudge-Improving-Decisions-Health-Happiness/dp/014311526X.

6. Kahneman, Daniel. 1982. Judgment Under Uncertainty: Heuristics and Biases. Edited by Paul Slovic, and Amos Tversky . 1st ed. Cambridge University Press. https://www.amazon.com/Judgment-Under-Uncertainty-Heuristics-Biases/dp/0521284147.

# 3

# Implementing a DMF Can Break the Doom Loop

**THE PERFORMANCE OF** any organization is ultimately a function of the quality of its members' decisions and their ability to execute on those decisions effectively. It's not rocket science, but the bottom line is that your organization's performance will suffer if your team makes more bad decisions than good ones. You could even get it right more than you get it wrong, but it may take only a few catastrophically wrong decisions to obliterate your organization. A 2013 Bain & Company study[7] quantified the financial impacts of good decision-making as follows:

> "Decision effectiveness and financial results correlate at a 95% confidence level or higher for every country, industry, and company size we studied. Top-quintile companies on decisions generate average total shareholder returns nearly six percentage points higher than those of other companies."

While decision-making skills are critical to an organization's success, few leaders say that their organizations are very good at making decisions. A 2019 McKinsey Survey[8] revealed that, "Only 20% of respondents say their organizations excel at decision-making. Further, a majority say that much of the time they devote to decision-making is used ineffectively."

What is remarkable, then, is that so few companies and leaders make improving their team's decision-making skills a specific goal or initiative. If you are a leader who recognizes the powerful impact you can make on your organization's

> **What is remarkable, then, is that so few companies and leaders make improving their team's decision-making skills a specific goal or initiative.**

performance by enabling your team to make better decisions, where should you start?

Another McKinsey study[9] provides an important insight:

> "After controlling for factors like industry, geography, and company size, we used regression analysis to calculate how much of the variance in decision outcomes was explained by the quality of the process and how much by the quantity and detail of the analysis. The answer: process mattered more than analysis—by a factor of six."

So, rather than focusing on more advanced analytical tools and technology, the data shows us that we must start by ensuring our team utilizes a sound decision-making process. This is why any leader who wants to empower their team to make better decisions must first enable them by adopting and implementing a common DMF that they and their team members will use for making and communicating decisions. This common DMF should be flexible so it can be used efficiently for relatively simple decisions, but can also be "scaled up" for more complex decisions. Furthermore, it should also be designed to mitigate the effects of decision traps.

Implementing and training your team on a common DMF can have the following benefits:

- Better, faster training: By adopting a single DMF and having the whole organization apply it, we can develop scalable training materials, classes, and interventions we can use to teach our teams how to apply the framework efficiently and effectively.

- Increased engagement in decision-making: When we all use a common DMF, we all know what the "next step" in the process is, and we are more able to jump in and back each other up.
- Streamlined communication: When we all use the same DMF and communicate our decision-making process using that framework, team members develop a common language that allows them to share their decisions more efficiently and effectively. Furthermore, communicating our decision-making process using a common framework allows leaders to give the team better feedback regarding the quality of the decision.

Allow me to share a real-life example of this last point. As we discussed earlier, one of the simplest and most effective techniques I have found to create a culture of empowerment within my teams is to ask people to give me a recommendation rather than ask me "what I want them to do." When I first started doing this, however, I got a lot of funny looks. Their recommendations often made little sense, and I felt like they just tried guessing what I wanted them to do. As a result, I spent an unsustainable amount of time talking through their decision-making process with them. The problem was that they needed more training or experience in making decisions and learning how to communicate their thought process.

However, once I taught the team a common DMF, I communicated the expectation that when they gave me their recommendation, they followed the steps of the DMF. This dramatically streamlined the conversation and added the benefit of forcing them to apply the DMF before they called me with their recommendation. For instance, one of the steps in our common DMF was to "Brainstorm Alternatives." I set the expectation that when someone called me for help with a decision or to request approval, that they followed the DMF; they knew that I expected to hear the alternatives they had considered without asking for them. This put the ownership on them and ensured they had at least tried to brainstorm alternatives before we discussed the issue while still providing me an opportunity to help back them up in case there were viable alternatives they hadn't considered.

The benefits of implementing a common DMF can be significant and widespread throughout an organization. And while it may be difficult to value one positive outcome over another depending on the industry you are in, we can probably all agree that revenue and profit are by far the most important bottom line metrics. Without cashflow, all operations would cease to function. Without positive cashflow, the organization would cease to exist. I saw this first hand at a facility I was tasked with overseeing in Dudley, North Carolina.

Over the previous few years, production had plummeted by thirty to forty percent compared to its previous performance levels. A once-profitable plant was now significantly underperforming and incurring losses. Upon arrival, I employed the same approach we will dissect in detail throughout this book. I would start by examining machinery, oftentimes encountering methods of operation that appeared illogical. When I asked the workers why they were proceeding in that specific manner, the responses frequently cited previous mandates from former plant management without any other insight or explanation. I would then inquire, if they had better ways in mind on how to handle this. They would share their insights, and we would evaluate the alternatives together, once again applying the same DMF. Within a mere six months, we had revitalized the plant, restoring production to its initial benchmarks and significantly improving overall operations.

Later on in my career, I joined Owens Corning and managed their largest residential fiberglass insulation plant for a few years. This was a very different environment from what I was used to in the military and beyond, given that it was a unionized facility. The union's presence, a force for the last fifty years, undoubtedly posed its challenges. Directly influencing frontline operators in a union setting is limited since we are operating on terms stipulated in the contract, not necessarily on company profitability. However, this did not stop me from applying the same principles of the framework by sharing it with the management team, encompassing the supervisors and managers. By adopting a similar approach, we achieved comparable success.

Following my tenure there, I joined a start-up consulting firm, Wilson Perumal & Company, where I established and developed an operational excellence practice. My focus was on teaching clients how to implement comprehensive integrated management systems. This practice grew into a successful venture, generating approximately five million dollars annually. It was there that I truly honed my approach. Although my previous roles involved altering the cultural dynamics of the three separate plants, I wouldn't characterize my methods as particularly systematic. The transformation was more a result of personal interactions and my leadership style rather than a formalized process. But the one thing that remained constant through all these experiences was the positive impact my DMF had on the bottom line.

## Benefits

A significant advantage of this framework is not only enhanced performance but also the speed at which we achieve these results. Enhanced performance in shorter time frames inherently yields better outcomes. When we take this a step further by educating the entire team on employing this uniform framework, the effect is compounded. Uniformity in process across the team means we are not just operating more effectively—we are also accelerating our pace, since we are all speaking the same strategic language instead of relying on one or a handful of leaders to speak the decision-making language.

This unified method streamlines our workflow and fosters a collaborative environment where decisions are made swiftly and implemented efficiently. It's the synchronization of our collective efforts that drives faster, high-quality results, ultimately contributing to improved metrics across the board. Whether those metrics consist of rising revenue figures, reduced safety violations, increased productivity, or reduced downtime due to less indecision, a standard DMF will greatly increase efficiency at all levels of the organization while freeing up time for senior leaders to use their time on more important, higher-level tasks.

> **This unified method streamlines our workflow and fosters a collaborative environment where decisions are made swiftly and implemented efficiently.**

Hopefully, your team is already receiving training in some capacity to help them become capable of supporting each other more effectively. However, the best training in the world does not address the root cause if it only focuses on technical skills and situation specific examples. It is clear that better performance stems from making better decisions. An equation I like using to represent this is:

**Decisions (X) Behaviors = Outcomes**

The decisions I make play a critical role in that equation. Even with the right behavior and strong execution, bad decisions will likely lead to poor results. Conversely, making good decisions is crucial for achieving positive outcomes. Standardizing the DMF and educating everybody on it enables our organization to attain those good results more efficiently and swiftly. And while poor results in general are not good at any level of an organization, those that impact safety can be the most damaging of all. It is possible to bounce back from a bad quarter of sales, but the damage done from bodily harm to your employees can quickly put you out of business.

After leaving Georgia Pacific, I advanced to become an equity partner at Wilson Perumal & Company. During that period, a company by the name of Enviva approached me to come on board in an operational role. At the time, Enviva was a company with annual revenues around $350 million. They operated four plants, each grappling with significant safety issues. The injury rate was alarmingly high, exceeding a value of three. This meant that for every hundred workers, three are seriously injured every year. As an employer of 450 employees, we were on pace to have 13 serious injuries per year. On top of this, they were facing annual property damage claims approximating $30 million, largely due to fires. Despite these challenges, the business was performing well financially, and there was an ambition to double the size of the business within the next five years.

The CEO and the EVP of Operations were acutely aware that achieving this level of growth was contingent upon introducing a greater degree of operational discipline and standardization across all four plants. The presence of disparate practices at each facility was not a scalable model and would quickly become a detractor to their growth plans. Acknowledging this, they recruited me to spearhead the improvement of safety procedures and to foster a cultural shift toward more rigorous management and operation of their plants. The goal was to infuse a spirit of operational discipline throughout their facilities.

For the initial years, I dedicated myself to taking on the roles of Head of safety, quality, environmental aspects, and the operational excellence group. The efforts paid off handsomely over that period and we managed to drive the incident rate down to a remarkable 0.32, which is considered world-class. In the last three years of my tenure, the company completely eliminated insurance claims resulting from fires. Buoyed by this success, I was promoted to oversee all operations. Under my leadership, the company experienced significant growth. We elevated the business from approximately $350 million in revenue to a striking $1.3 billion, expanded the operations from four to ten plants, and managed four ports. The series of achievements under my direction spoke volumes of the success we had. The improved decision-making processes proved that safety need not be compromised to increase profitability.

Another specific example of how the DMF proved transformational involved our handling of downtime events.

For instance, if a major conveyor or key piece of equipment failed and took the entire plant offline in the process, it understandably caught the attention of top management. Naturally, the CEO would be on the line with me and the EVP of Operations, wanting updates.

"When will the plant be operational again? When will the equipment be repaired?" I would inquire of the plant manager, who might optimistically estimate a six-hour repair time. However, six hours would pass, then twelve. Before you knew it the day was lost, the plant remained inactive, and profitability diminished.

Upon follow-up, the response might echo the initial estimate: "It'll be up in another six hours," they would say, triggering a sense of déjà vu.

"Wait a minute, that's the same time frame you provided yesterday, right?" It was like they had gotten into the habit of randomly throwing out timeframes and hoping for the best without having a concrete plan in place to make sure it was attainable.

Such recurring scenarios underscored the need for a more accurate and reliable approach to problem-solving and communication. The immediate proposal to address the issue was to initiate hourly phone calls with the plant in an effort to closely monitor and manage the repair progress. While this approach led to a slight improvement, the overall impact was marginal and did not fundamentally resolve the challenges we were facing. Furthermore, this method of micromanagement created a dreadful experience for everyone involved. It was clear that continuous status checks were not the optimal solution we needed for effective and efficient problem resolution. Recognizing that the approach of conducting hourly updates led to excessive micromanagement and hindered the morale of our leaders, I opted for a strategic shift in response to major equipment failures.

Instead of persistent phone calls, I suggested the plant managers should convene with their teams immediately after a significant breakdown. Their task was to methodically consider all repair alternatives and conduct a thorough analysis to determine the most viable solution. Once a plan was established, they were to predict the best-case timeline for the repairs, detailing the factors that would need to align for this to be achievable. They also had to prepare for the worst-case scenario, examining the potential issues that could prolong the process. The plant managers were then to lay out specific actions aimed at ensuring that positive outcomes were realized and pitfalls were avoided. This plan, along with the best and worst-case timeline, was to be sent to me in writing.

I decided to eliminate the update calls completely. After the repair work concluded, we would reconvene to evaluate our performance against the predicted time frames and analyze the effectiveness of our planning and execution. This proactive and structured approach was intended to promote efficiency and accountability, without succumbing to the drawbacks of micromanagement. The impact of shifting to this proactive plan-driven strategy was immediate and significant. Not only were the plants reviving operations within the projected time frames, but we also consistently neared the best-case timelines—a marked improvement from our previous endeavors. This advancement took place in the absence of relentless micromanagement, demonstrating that empowering teams with the right tools and autonomy could yield superior results.

This transformational experience was instrumental in the creation of the "best case-worst case" sheet, which we will cover in more detail in Chapter 9. This tool laid the groundwork for a more efficient and collaborative problem-solving environment. That experience is really the essence of my journey which led to starting Enabling Empowerment. The impetus came as Enviva grew into a publicly traded company. I felt it was time for me to move on and explore new opportunities. During my career, I've seen many consultants and various experts who can help with improving problem-solving skills or conducting specific analyses within portions of a DMF. What I observed to be missing from the marketplace was a consulting firm that could provide leaders with both the culture transformation strategies and the tools and training necessary to break the Micromanagement Doom Loop and truly empower their teams.

## Scalability of Training

If I'm the leader of an organization and I express the need to improve our DMF, execution, and results, I have two very different options I could employ. Let's say I have five direct reports, all of whom are the heads of their respective divisions with dozens if not hundreds of people in their organizational chart. We all come to the agreement that we need to enhance the decision-making process in their individual divisions for the greater good of the organization. The first option would be for us to collaborate on one large scale framework we could collectively roll out to each division under their direct supervision. The second option would be for each of these leaders to own the training for their own division independent of the others, regardless of whether that meant creating five different curricula or bringing in five different consultants.

In the absence of a single, unified approach to teaching decision-making, I would be opening the door for potential chaos. We would be talking about five different processes, five different consultants, and five different costs of training. And for what? Each department would be doing things their own way with no regard for how the others do it, making it impossible for any type of cross-company collaboration. It might not seem so bad with only five departments, but with each additional department doing whatever they want, the likelihood for disconnects grows.

When each department agrees to adopt a unified framework, it puts everyone on the same page and makes them feel like they are on the same team. Someone from Department A could fill in for someone in Department B and still be able to apply the same decision-making skills they would have used in their own department to achieve the same results. This approach is scalable, allowing for easy implementation and leverage across the board. When we teach it, an employee moving from one group to another won't face the hassle of learning new methods; they can simply carry on as they were in their previous group. This is the advantage of having a common system—instead of each leader independently instructing their team, we devise shared tools and decision-making strategies that are consistently used throughout the organization.

As we progressed and expanded during my tenure at Enviva, the consideration for scaling how we trained employees became crucial. Upon my arrival, all key decisions—be it the installation of equipment or allocation of capital—were only made by the most senior leadership. More often than not, plant personnel were simply informed of projects as they were being implemented without having the opportunity to provide any input. Along the way, it became clear that a senior leader might not possess all the answers, particularly as the number of plants increased from four to ten. Such a system, inherently flawed, could not sustain with the expansion, so I strove to shift this approach.

It was essential for those at the plant level to engage in these decisions actively. They needed to be able to approach the leadership and offer guidance on where the company should invest, leveraging their detailed operational knowledge and expertise. I invested considerable time in educating plant leadership teams and engineers on our DMF, as well as strengthening their financial analysis capabilities. During one of the years under my stewardship, I assumed control over the maintenance capital budget. As we entered that fiscal year, the requests for capital expenditure were double the available budget.

Realizing the impracticability of the situation, I convened with the project managers. I insisted that, before progressing any further, they needed a solid understanding of our decision-making process. I led them through the framework and trained them in conducting financial analyses using ranges of potential outcomes, rather than relying on single-point estimates where we were shooting for one specific number or metric. The transformation to the business was profound. Almost immediately, the amount of capital being requested halved as the teams recognized more efficient methods and solutions beyond the initial requests for funding.

Previously, the typical request sounded something like, "I need $500,000 to fix this issue." When I probed for alternatives that had been considered, the answers were often limited. "We could choose not to fix it," they might say. When I made them think a little further as to what the implications of not fixing the issue could be, I would get responses like: "If we don't fix it, the plant could deteriorate."

This led to an opportunity for further education. "Let's revisit this," I would suggest. "I'll show you how to properly frame a problem, assess risks, and weigh benefits." Through this instruction, we began receiving much more refined requests for capital expenditures. This allowed us to make more strategic decisions and remain within our budget constraints, maximizing the use of our available funds.

## How to Implement a Common DMF

Implementing a common DMF is not going to happen overnight. The leader is likely already caught in the Micromanagement Doom Loop and does not have the time to do anything but continue to pull people out of the lake. For the DMF to be effective, the organization must put an emphasis on training their people on how to make and implement those decisions. Where organizations tend to go wrong is by assuming it should be the leader who is responsible for providing this training. If they had the time, most would like nothing more than to empower their people and free up time in their day—but they don't have the time.

This first became apparent to me when I was managing a plant with more than 400 people reporting to me on a daily basis. The routine response to any decision out of the norm was to come to the boss for an answer. If even ten percent of those employees needed help making a decision on any given day, I was already out of time and likely to not only miss some critical issues but also not have the time to do my own job. While I would have liked nothing more than to coach each employee on a one-to-one basis so they could learn and become more independent, it just wasn't a viable option. What I needed was a strategy.

I started pulling thirty-to-forty people into a classroom at a time to teach them. This allowed for the business to continue running while we upskilled approximately ten percent of the workforce at any one time. This helped tremendously, but it was not a permanent solution either. No one retains everything they learn in a classroom setting, especially if it is not reinforced afterward. Coaching and oversight are still very much required, and to attempt that on an "as-needed" basis will only result in burnout for the leader and failure for the employee. This is where I find third-party resources like independent consultants and courses to be helpful and effective.

To get a better understanding of what the 7 Step DMF looks like before we dive into a detailed analysis of each individual step, the graphic below should get you acclimated with what to expect:

THE DECISION-MAKING FRAMEWORK REFERENCE GUIDE

| | Key Questions/Actions | Decision Traps to Avoid | Tools to Use |
|---|---|---|---|
| Define Opportunity and Objectives | • Write a statement that defines the opportunity...not the solution<br>• Determine the "size of the prize" | • Framing Trap<br>• Curse of Knowledge<br>• Risk Aversion, Conservatism<br>• Opportunity Cost | • Problem/Opportunity Framing Tip Sheet<br>• Prioritized List of Opportunities |
| Develop a Range of Creative Alternatives | • Brainstorm ways the opportunity could be captured<br>• List pros/cons of each idea<br>• Narrow down list to top 3 or 4 ideas | • Anchoring Trap<br>• Halo Effect<br>• Status-quo Trap | • Brainstorming Tip Sheet<br>• Optimized Base Case Tip Sheet |
| Identify Key Drivers | • Identify the Key Drivers of success<br>• What are the 3 to 4 variables that drive 80% of the outcome? | • Base-Rate Neglect & WYSIATI<br>• Representativeness<br>• Availability Bias | • Business Driver Cause-Effect Map<br>• Sensitivity Analysis<br>• 80/20 Rule |
| Manage Risk and Upside | • Determine the full range of outcomes for each of the Key Drivers<br>• What is the best and the worst outcome for each Driver? | • Law of Small Numbers<br>• Overconfidence<br>• Confirmation Bias | • Key Driver Upside/Downside Table<br>• Post-Mortem Tip Sheet<br>• Outside View/Red Teaming |
| Perform Economic Analysis | • Calculate cashflow and return on investment for each alternative and the upside/downside case | • Diminishing Returns<br>• Sunk Costs<br>• Time Value of Money | • Economic Analysis Models |
| Determine Required Capabilities and | • Identify what capabilities will be needed to implement<br>• What is the next step and who owns it?<br>• How will we measure progress? | • Planning Fallacy<br>• Comparative Advantage | • Best Case/Worst Case Plan and Milestones<br>• Segmentation<br>• Reference Class Forecasting |
| Show Your Work | • Document your decision-making framework<br>• Validate the actual results | • Hindsight Bias<br>• Desirability Trap | • DMF Summary Template<br>• DMF Discussion Reminder Card |

Step 1 is where we will define the opportunity and objectives as they relate to any decisions you want to ensure are handled more effectively in the future. The key in this step is not focusing on a solution. Too many people jump straight to finding an answer without taking the time to clearly understand where the opportunity lies and the various ways that may exist to arrive at our desired end state.

In Step 2, we will develop a range of creative alternatives to the way things are currently being handled in your organization. What we don't want to do here is cherry pick only what we think could be the best or most impactful ideas and options. There should be a true collaborative brainstorming process where absolutely everything that comes to mind is written down along with any associated pros and cons for each thought. Only when every single idea has been generated should you move on to whittling the list down to the top three or four ideas.

When you get to Step 3, it is time to identify the key drivers of success for your chosen initiative. This is important because not all influencing factors are created equal and it can be easy to get caught up spending time focusing on the wrong things. The drivers responsible for the most significant impact should be prioritized above all others. As a rule of thumb, try focusing on only the top drivers that will contribute 80% or more of the results to your desired outcome.

Step 4 is all about managing both the risks, the downside, and the rewards, the upsides. Much like you brainstormed ideas in Step 2, it is advisable here to list the full range of outcomes, both negative and positive, that could result from each of the key drivers identified in the previous step. You can then decide what the best case and worst case outcomes would be after they are implemented. Looking only at the best or worst without accounting for the opposite end of the spectrum can lead to a skewed reality of risks and rewards.

Performing Economic Analysis in Step 5 all boils down to the money. In most organizations these positives and negatives will likely be evaluated on a dollars and cents basis. Senior leaders are going to want to know how much money stands to be made or lost with each new decision being made so they mitigate what is acceptable and what is not. The positive or negative cashflow generated by each of the best and worst case examples will allow leadership to determine if the level of risk is acceptable.

By Step 6, we move on to determining the required capabilities and next steps the organization will need to take to move forward with the initiative. It is likely that many of the options under consideration and the associated key drivers will require some sort of resource that can all boil down to time, money, or both. Once you are confident you have the capabilities to proceed, each next step needs to be assigned to a responsible party with clear action steps on what is to come next along with a way to measure the progress they make (or don't).

Finally, in Step 7, we show our work. That is a just a fancy way of saying that someone needs to document the DMF from beginning to end so that anyone who was not involved in the ideation process can follow a logical train of thought and replicate the process easily enough. Then you validate that the results are actually what were intended.

7. Blenko, Marcia W., Michael C. Mankins, and Paul Rogers. "Decision Insights." Bain & Company. November 20, 2013. https://media.bain.com/Images/DECISION%20INSIGHTS_Compendium_Issues1-5.pdf.

8. De Smet, Aaron, Iskandar Aminov, Gregor Jost, and David Mendelsoh. "Decision Making in the Age of Urgency." McKinsey & Company. April 1, 2019. https://www.mckinsey.com/capabilities/people-and-organizational-performance/our-insights/decision-making-in-the-age-of-urgency#/.

9. Lovallo, Dan, and Olivier Sibony. "The Case for Behavioral Strategy." McKinsey & Company. March 1, 2010. https://www.mckinsey.com/capabilities/strategy-and-corporate-finance/our-insights/the-case-for-behavioral-strategy.

# The 7-Steps of the Decision-Making Framework

# 4

# Step 1 - Define Opportunity & Objective

**AS WITH MOST** systems, processes, and frameworks, the first step is the most important. The first step of defining the opportunity and objective in my DMF is no different. Defining the opportunity and objective sets the stage for everything that will follow; from the time and resources invested all the way up to measuring results and determining success. At times, the opportunity, or problem, may be crystal clear on the surface. But there will be times where all you can see are symptoms of the problem or opportunity and you will need to perform root cause analysis to determine exactly what it is you are trying to solve for. And the key here is speaking only in terms of the opportunity, not potential solutions to what you *think* may be the pain point in the organization.

Before moving on to the next part of this step, we need to determine the size of the prize. Just because you may have clearly defined the opportunity you want to solve for does not necessarily make it the most valuable use of your time and resources. From my experience, there have been countless times where employees will bring forth an opportunity that could make or save the organization a hundred dollars when there are other opportunities right beneath the surface worth hundreds of thousands of dollars. And even if the hundred dollar opportunity really is the only one at hand, but the time and capital investment is going to cost far more than doing nothing, it might be best to look for other opportunities.

**A good opportunity statement will allow for more than one answer and foster an environment of dialogue and creativity where multiple people can weigh in on potential solutions.**

If the size of the prize indicates the opportunity is worth solving for, you can now test your opportunity statement with different people. A good opportunity statement will allow for more than one answer and foster an environment of dialogue and creativity where multiple people can weigh in on potential solutions. Take a second to look at the graphic below, where the left column offers bad problem statements with only a limited number of options and the right column is much more open ended.

| Bad Problem Statement | Better Problem Statement |
|---|---|
| I need a new house | The ratio of stuff to space in my house is too high |
| I need a new car | The reliability/cost of my car is too low/high |
| I need a raise | I can't cover my expenses |
| I need more people | I need to reduce the ratio of work to resources |

The first statement of "I need a new house" only offers two potential solutions. You can either buy a new house, or stay living in the same house. To determine which of those decisions is right, we need more information. If the reason for thinking you need a new house is because the ratio of stuff you own in relation to the amount of space you have is too high, then you have considerably more options. You can sell some of the stuff, donate it to charity, rent a storage unit, or possibly buy a new house. The same could be said with the second poorly framed problem statement about needing a new car. If reliability is the real issue, maybe a tune-up would suffice. Or maybe you would find that reliable access to public transportation means you don't need a car at all.

Once you think you have crafted a well-thought-out problem statement that does not limit your choices to option A or option B, test it with different people. See if they can think of other potential solutions to whatever you have described, and if they think the problem is worth solving. And don't just stop at one problem statement. Identify as many as possible and maintain a prioritized list of those opportunities, along with a hurdle rate to specify a specific threshold for the rate of return on a particular investment. The hurdle rate in these instances is significant because it provides a baseline for decision-makers to know in advance if a particular opportunity is even worth elevating to upper management.

For example, a company may have a policy in place stipulating that any acquisition or project must demonstrate a potential for at least a ten percent internal rate of return. In practical terms, this means if the anticipated return on an investment falls below this hurdle rate, the proposal should not be brought forward for discussion, no matter what the potential dollar amount of the gain or savings is. This threshold acts as a gatekeeper, ensuring that only the most financially promising investments consume the company's time and resources. The hurdle rate acts as a filter to sift through potential initiatives. It serves as a practical mechanism to separate viable ideas from those that are less likely to be profitable. And it's not limited to the internal rate of return alone.

For instance, imagine walking into a manufacturing plant with the intention of brainstorming cost-saving measures. The hurdle rate could be applied in this context as well—not only in terms of financial returns, but also in evaluating the efficacy and potential savings of those proposed ideas. To drive cost-saving initiatives, we encourage everyone to bring their ideas to the table. However, we have established a minimum hurdle rate for consideration. If an idea doesn't yield at least $10,000 in annual savings, we prefer not to discuss it at this time.

The purpose of this strategy is to filter out less impactful suggestions and to provide clear guidance on our priorities. Clearly, there may be situations where an idea could save $20,000 a year and, due to its simplicity and ease of implementation, we might prioritize it over another that could save $100,000 a year. The less complex initiative could be executed immediately, while the more significant savings could be deferred. Nevertheless, if a proposal is only expected to save $5,000, it falls below our threshold regardless of how easy it would be to implement. We aim to focus our efforts on opportunities with a larger financial impact.

## Framing Trap

The Framing Trap occurs when our decisions are influenced by the way in which information is presented to us. To make the best decisions, we need to frame problems and opportunities in a way that helps us identify as many creative alternatives as possible. To best understand how the framing trap appears and how it can impact your ability to make a quick but accurate decision, let's take a simple quiz.

How do you pronounce the capital of Kentucky? Is it pronounced:

A: Louisville, like Lewisville or
B: Louisville, like Leweyville

Have you got your answer? The correct answer is:

The capital of Kentucky is pronounced like Frankfort.

Be honest. You at least thought about whether the answer was A or B. And if you did—welcome to the majority. You just found yourself to be the newest victim of the framing trap. I've asked this question to hundreds of people over the years, and even people from the state of Kentucky have proudly defended either A or B as their answer, only to be dismayed when I reminded them it was Frankfort.

The Framing Trap occurs when our decisions are influenced by the way in which information is presented to us. If you are wondering how often that actually happens in life, I have a newsflash for you, because it always happens. You may think I am over-exaggerating to prove a point, and if so, indulge me a little further. Here are a few examples of how framing affects our everyday decisions:

**The Framing Trap occurs when our decisions are influenced by the way in which information is presented to us.**

1. If two yogurt brands are identical in every way, but one is described as 80% fat-free, and the other is described as 20% fat, which one would you buy?
2. Are you more likely to positively accept feedback from your leader on an "opportunity for improvement" or a "performance issue"?
3. Would you choose to undergo a medical procedure with a 90% success rate? What about one with a 10% failure rate?

How a problem or opportunity is framed may be the most influential factor in our DMF. Throughout my career as an operations executive, I've experienced the Framing Trap many times when I'm presented with a recommendation that is essentially a binary choice between either spending money on X or not spending money on X. And, of course, the consequences of not spending money on X are totally unacceptable, so I really have no choice but to approve the request. These discussions usually devolved into a debate over whether the assertions about X were true or whether the severity of the consequences of not doing X were realistic.

**How a problem or opportunity is framed may be the most influential factor in our DMF.**

Frankly, they weren't very productive discussions and usually ended with the requestor feeling like I wasn't listening and me feeling like they were too lazy to come up with other alternatives. I could not wrap my head around how any decision could only be evaluated on an either A or B, X or no X, yes or no basis. However, once I understood the Framing Trap, I could turn these conversations into a fruitful dialog that resulted in collaboration and frequently led to breakthrough ideas. I realized no one was being lazy; they just didn't know how to frame the problem in a way that led to anything other than a binary choice.

Here are some tips for framing problems or opportunities in a way that will help your team identify more creative alternatives.

1. Understand the problem: Go see the problem (GEMBA) and interview a variety of stakeholders working where the value is created. Gemba is a Japanese term loosely translated as the "real" or "actual" place, and in business the value is generally created

on the shop floor or the sales floor. Identify areas for improvement and work to implement them by encouraging transparency, trust, and communication between leaders and workers.

2. Identify the "Size of the Prize": What is it worth to solve this problem or capture this opportunity? How does it compare to other opportunities? How should it be prioritized?

3. Perform Root Cause Analysis: Identify and understand the problem's root causes. Address the causes, not the symptoms.

4. Develop your initial Problem/Opportunity Statement: If you start with a problem, try reframing it as an opportunity. Ask yourself the following questions. If the answer is yes to any, keep working.

   - Does the problem appear to have only one possible solution?
   - Does the statement lead to too many possible solutions?
   - Does the statement describe a symptom instead of the problem?
   - Does the statement suggest the problem is that you don't have enough time, money, or people?

Another way to avoid the framing trap is to test your framing with others:

1. Get feedback from various stakeholders, including decision-makers, end users, and front-line employees.

2. Don't automatically accept the initial frame, whether it was formulated by you or someone else. Always

try to reframe the problem in various ways. Look for distortions caused by the frames.

3. When others recommend decisions, examine the way they framed the problem. Challenge them with different frames.

## Curse of Knowledge

We often hear the expression that "knowledge is power," but what if I were to tell you that it can also be a curse that leads to one of the most common decision traps in the first step of the DMF? It can be difficult being the smartest person in the room when no one else understands what you are trying to convey to them. That is because a knowledgeable person, be it themselves or someone else, cannot accurately reconstruct what a person, without the same level of knowledge, would think or how they would act. Have you ever played poker with someone who doesn't know how to play? Sure, after enough hands they will come to understand the basic mechanics. But chances are they will not only significantly slow the pace of the game but also likely lose money in the process.

To demonstrate the Curse of Knowledge decision trap, let's look at a question from a test given to kindergarteners, likely in a spelling or grammar class, where they are asked to alphabetize words. The expectation for most might be to do so by arranging the words based on the beginning letter for each. However, look at how this kindergartener approached the task. Instead of alphabetizing the words, the student alphabetized the letters within each word.

C. Write these words in **alphabetical order.**

1. take        _a e k t_

   value       _a e l u v_

   use         _e s u_

2. royal       _a l o r y_

When you start to think about it, if you have never encountered this exercise before or seen it demonstrated, it's perfectly reasonable to interpret the assignment in that way, right? This conundrum, or "Curse of Knowledge," is the paradox of expertise. Once we acquire specific information or have undergone certain experiences, such as the task of alphabetizing words, it becomes somewhat difficult for us to truly comprehend how someone without that background might interpret our directions.

In essence, our expertise blinds us—it is virtually impossible to disregard what we already understand. The concept that "you cannot unknow what you know" applies here. This realization holds significant importance in various aspects of communication and teaching. When we dissect a problem or explore a potential opportunity, our intrinsic understanding might cloud our ability to see things from a fresh perspective. As a result, when we engage with others regarding a problem or opportunity, we must bear in mind they might not share our level of insight or expertise.

> **When we dissect a problem or explore a potential opportunity, our intrinsic understanding might cloud our ability to see things from a fresh perspective.**

Therefore, it is essential for us to exercise empathy and patience. Try to put yourself in someone's shoes, making a concerted effort to see through their lens. Only by doing so can we truly grasp how they perceive the situation, which in turn enables us to communicate our knowledge and intentions more effectively. Related to this finding is the phenomenon experienced by players of charades: the actor may find it frustratingly hard to believe that their teammates keep failing to guess the secret phrase, known only to the actor, conveyed by pantomime. If you ever played the game and been in the role of the person who needs to help your teammates guess what you are describing, then you know exactly what this feels like. You know the word once you begin drawing or acting and now you cannot unknow it. This knowledge then makes you question why no one else shares the same knowledge with you.

From a business perspective, I vividly remember one lesson from a supervisor in my career. His assertion was that "two reasonable people given the same set of facts will generally come to the same conclusion on the correct course of action." So, if you and I do not agree, my initial assumption should not be that you are unreasonable but rather that we do not have the same set of facts. Maybe I have certain details you do not, or vice versa. The first step in working toward an agreement would be to compare the information we both have access to and confirm it is the same. If it is, and we are still unable to come to the same conclusion, then we must assume one or both of us is being unreasonable.

> **"Two reasonable people given the same set of facts will generally come to the same conclusion on the correct course of action."**

## Risk Aversion & Conservatism

While Risk Aversion and Conservatism are not exactly the same thing based on Kahneman's definitions, they are closely linked enough to cover them as part of the same decision trap. The key concept here is that framing a problem as an opportunity to realize a gain or experience a loss influences how people approach any given situation. From a risk aversion standpoint, it would be safe to say that the large majority of the population lean more in that direction than those who embrace risk. Conservatism is more the mindset behind why we either seek out risk or avoid it.

In a risk-averse decision situation, the person in charge of calling the shots is going to be presented with two different ways of looking at the same outcome. Let's say a plant manager just discovers that a particular machine is malfunctioning. There are already raw materials on the assembly line, products in the finishing stage, and others rolling off and moving to packing and shipping. They are told that if they don't shut the production down immediately, there is a risk of losing 25% of the work in process. However, the person delivering that message fails to mention that while this 25% loss is true, continuing to run the machine for another thirty minutes will result in 50% of the product near the end of the assembly line successfully reaching completion.

The two decisions are not mutually exclusive. If the manager chooses to keep the machine running, they are certain to lose the 25% of the raw materials used in production, but also ensure the 50% completion that would otherwise be lost. What is more valuable in this situation: saving 25% of raw material or ensuring the completion of 50% of the saleable goods? If you are thinking that's a great question, you are on the right track. There really is no way of answering that question without having more context, which is what makes this decision trap so dangerous. Additional questions that could be asked before making a decision are:

- How much time has been invested into the 50% we can complete?
- What percentage of the raw material is accounted for in the 50% we would ultimately lose anyway if we shut the machines down immediately?
- Do we have time-sensitive pending orders for the finished product that will result in damaged relationships and potential cancellations?

These questions could go on forever, but the point is the same. An aversion to risk could prompt a decision-maker to act hastily in favor of the option that does not have any "loss" associated with it, while overlooking the potential for gain realized by way of the loss. To make that even clearer, imagine you are a marine property adjuster charged with minimizing the loss of cargo on three insured barges that sank yesterday off the coast of Alaska. Each barge holds $200,000 worth of cargo, which will be lost if not salvaged within 72 hours. The owner of a local marine-salvage company gives you two options, both of which will cost the same:

> **An aversion to risk could prompt a decision-maker to act hastily in favor of the option that does not have any "loss" associated with it, while overlooking the potential for gain realized by way of the loss.**

**Plan A:** This plan will save the cargo of one of the three barges, worth $200,000.

**Plan B:** This plan has a one-third probability of saving the cargo on all three barges, worth $600,000, but has a two-thirds probability of saving nothing.

Which plan would you choose?

If you are like 71% of the respondents in the study, you chose the "less risky" Plan A, which will save one barge for sure. Another group in the study, however, was asked to choose between alternatives C and D:

**Plan C:** This plan will result in the loss of two of the three cargoes, worth $400,000.

**Plan D:** This plan has a two-thirds probability of resulting in the loss of all three cargoes and the entire $600,000 but has a one-third probability of losing no cargo.

Faced with this choice, 80% of these respondents preferred Plan D. The concept of risk aversion led the respondents to overlook the two-thirds chance of losing all the cargo because the opportunity existed to recover everything and walk away with $600,000.

Through the lens of conservatism, the same problem can also elicit very different responses when frames use different reference points. Let's say you are asked the following question:

Would you accept a fifty-fifty chance of either losing $300 or winning $500?

Regardless of whether you said yes or no to that question, pretend you were asked this question:

You have $2,000 in your checking account. Would you prefer to keep your checking account balance of $2,000 or to accept a fifty-fifty chance of having either $1,700 or $2,500 in your account?

Once again, the two questions pose the same problem. While your answers to both questions should, rationally speaking, be the same, studies have shown that many people would refuse the fifty-fifty chance in the first question but accept it in the second. Their different reactions result from the different reference points presented in the two frames. The first frame, with its reference point of zero, emphasizes incremental gains and losses, and the thought of losing triggers a conservative response in many people's minds. The second frame, with its reference point of $2,000, puts things into perspective by emphasizing the real financial impact of the decision.

In combating this decision trap, we must realize that sometimes, the devil is in the details. We are inclined to insert our opinions, experiences, or frames of reference that we think will help the other person in the decision-making process. Instead of falling victim to that trap, and needless extra work, try posing problems in a neutral, redundant way that combines gains and losses or embraces different reference points. Think hard throughout your decision-making process about the framing of the problem. At points throughout the process, particularly near the end, ask yourself how your thinking might change if the framing changed. When others recommend decisions, examine the way they framed the problem. Challenge them with different frames.

## Opportunity Cost

The concept of opportunity cost presents a common pitfall—failing to consider what you are sacrificing by choosing one option over others. This is so important early on in the decision-making process because it can cause shortsightedness that overlooks better options by ignoring the size of the prize. Many organizations, when trying to identify possible improvements, do not systematically evaluate the potential rewards associated with each of their numerous opportunities. Without doing this, there is a tendency to pursue less valuable opportunities at the expense of those with higher value.

Consider a scenario where we are focused on an opportunity that is anticipated to save us $10,000 annually. While this might seem beneficial, we also have a separate opportunity that presents a much more significant potential gain—up to a million dollars per year. The question then arises: Why are we dedicating our resources and time to the opportunity with a comparatively modest return when there is another opportunity with the capacity to yield a hundred times that value? It is a matter of prioritization and strategic decision-making.

Realistically, it is impossible to act on every idea that comes our way each day. Therefore, making informed choices about where to direct our efforts is essential for maximizing returns and achieving greater success. Choosing a select number of impactful ideas is often more advantageous than trying to pursue every single suggestion. This becomes apparent when organizations encourage their teams to be proactive and contribute innovative ways to enhance business operations and overall organizational efficiency.

> **Making informed choices about where to direct our efforts is essential for maximizing returns and achieving greater success.**

In response, a plethora of ideas are typically put forward. Leaders then face the task of sifting through these numerous proposals—a task that, while important, can become overwhelming. They are faced with all these ideas, and instinctively, they might know certain ideas will not contribute significantly to their objectives. The difficulty lies not in the identification of these less impactful suggestions but in effectively communicating their lower priority status to the team without discouragement. To navigate this, a helpful strategy involves a proactive assessment of the idea by the person that suggested it in the first place. When a team member comes forward with a suggestion, they are also tasked with providing an appraisal of its potential value or impact—a concept often referred to as the "size of the prize."

For instance, if an employee presents an idea they believe might result in a $10,000 increase in revenue or cost savings, this estimation allows the idea to be weighed against others. If, among the slew of ideas pitched, this one ranks at the bottom in terms of estimated value, the decision not to pursue it becomes transparent and easier to understand. The team can clearly see why certain ideas are sidelined in favor of others with a larger perceived impact, helping to maintain focus on initiatives that promise the highest returns. This method ensures that not only are ideas evaluated in a logical and data-driven manner, but also the rationale for their selection or rejection is openly communicated and sensible to all the team members.

## Best Practices to Incorporate

Visit www.enablingempowerment.com to download these tools
- Problem/Opportunity Framing Tip Sheet
- Prioritized List of Opportunities

5

# Step 2 - Develop a Creative Range of Alternatives

**BECAUSE WE WERE** so effective in defining the opportunity, this next step becomes much more involved and moves us beyond the either/or decision. The slate of possibilities is completely blank and it becomes an interactive team task to fill it. Brainstorming sessions are particularly important at this stage because it allows for the free flow of ideas without judgment or decision. Each person involved in the decision-making process should write all their ideas down independently of one another to avoid deliberation until everyone has come up with everything they can think of. The importance of this cannot be overstated as you will likely be surprised by just how many more ideas are generated when the focus is on brainstorming and not discussion.

Once each collaborator has their list, you can go around the room and ask for everyone to share all the ideas on their list without judgment or opinion. The goal of this step is to make sure all potential solutions are voiced. After all of these potential solutions are on the table, talk through each of them, weighing the pros and cons of each as uncovered in the group conversation. Only after each person feels as if their list has been given thoughtful consideration should the leaders and influencers share their lists of suggestions. These potential opportunities should also be rated on the potential pros and cons regardless of who the person is.

Have a criteria as to how potential opportunities are going to be graded, ranked, or evaluated, so everyone knows why a particular suggestion made it further along in the process than some others. The goal is to whittle down the long lists each contributor came up with to the three or four most attractive opportunities for consideration among the group, no matter who came up with them. The goal is not to be the person with the winning idea, although it doesn't hurt, but to foster meaningful conversation by sharing open and honest feedback about all of the ideas that were circulated. Any potential solution that makes it beyond this step will be subjected to further scrutiny and evaluation in the next step of the decision-making framework.

To effectively navigate through some of the decision-making pitfalls we explore shortly, I implement two critical strategies. First, to sidestep the anchoring trap, I encourage everyone to independently jot down their own idea. This approach is particularly useful when I solicit input on generating solutions for a problem or ideas to capitalize on an opportunity. I might say something like, "All right, team, we need to come up with innovative ideas to tackle this issue or seize this chance. Let's all take a moment to independently record our thoughts."

This method ensures the group's input isn't swayed by an initial suggestion that could unfairly influence subsequent ideas—an occurrence that is quite common with anchoring. By collecting everyone's independent thoughts first, we ensure a diverse range of ideas without the undue influence of a single, potentially dominant perspective—such as one from a senior leader. It's a straightforward yet effective way to cultivate a broader and more balanced array of potential solutions. I will give them five minutes to capture their immediate, unfiltered thoughts without any external influence.

Once the five minutes are up, we'll go around the room, but I'll ask the most junior or less influential participants to share their ideas first. This strategy helps us to circumvent the halo effect and focus on those whose voices might otherwise be overshadowed, ensuring a fair and balanced consideration of all contributions. After everyone has carefully listened to the less influential voices, we can move on to the more experienced and higher level employees without fear of censorship where others could feel inclined to discard their original thoughts. This reluctance could be compounded by a desire to align with the more influential individual's perspective to appear in agreement. That's why it's crucial to have everyone articulate their thoughts without the pre-emptive influence of dominant voices.

To counteract this, I insist all participants read aloud every idea they've written down. It's natural that some ideas may seem less compelling as the discussion unfolds, and some may choose to self-censor, thinking their input is insignificant in retrospect. However, the mere act of writing down their ideas first ensures that these thoughts are given a chance to surface. Having gathered our list and generating perhaps fifteen to twenty different ideas, our next step is to evaluate them together. We'll openly discuss which ideas might be less feasible—those that appear clearly unworkable at this stage can be eliminated immediately. This is a process of collectively refining our list, aiming to narrow it down to four or five robust ideas that merit thorough discussion. We'll focus on these selected few that show the most promise for practical implementation or indicate significant potential benefits.

Then, we also have the concept of an "optimized base case," which serves as an essential benchmark in our operations.

It's defined by achieving the most favorable outcome with the resources currently available, that is, without the necessity of allocating significant extra funds. By adopting this optimized base case approach, our objective is not merely to understand our existing operational capacity, but to also establish a sturdy foundation for subsequent economic evaluations. This parameter is vital because, when we progress to the stage of conducting a detailed economic analysis, every alternative we consider needs to be scrutinized against this baseline. The rationale is straightforward: we need to measure the relative value and efficiency of potential investments accurately.

To give a concrete example, suppose our current set-up enables us to manufacture 100 units daily, and we don't have to loosen the purse strings any further for that level of production. Now, imagine we're assessing the option of acquiring a new piece of machinery that promises an output of 120 units per day. In this scenario, our economic analysis will pivot on quantifying and assessing the additional investment required to secure that incremental production of units per day. We'll examine whether the financial outlay for this additional capacity is justified and if it positions us for better long-term efficiency and profitability.

**The term "optimized base case" is critical because it refers to the most efficient operation of our current assets without additional significant investments.**

The term "optimized base case" is critical because it refers to the most efficient operation of our current assets without additional significant investments. I've often noticed situations where a piece of equipment, for instance, is allowed to fall into disrepair—take a machine that breaks down every three months due to inadequate maintenance, such as not being properly lubricated. The knee-jerk reaction might be to purchase a new machine for a million dollars, assuming it will generate a positive return on investment by avoiding breakdowns. However, the logical step before such an investment is simply maintaining the equipment we already own. Rather than buying new, we should be lubricating our current machine.

We should not establish our base case on poor practices or neglect. We can't justify investing in new solutions to cover up habitual errors. The optimized base case should reflect the peak performance of our existing operations with correct maintenance, not a history of lapses. Only then can we make a sound comparison when considering upgrades or additional investments.

The concept of an "optimized base case" can be somewhat challenging to apply, and while it might seem out of context at initial stages of a project, it becomes particularly relevant during the economic analysis phase. Over time, I've encountered questions regarding the incorporation of safety improvements into cost assessments. Specifically, there are concerns about whether a monetary value should be assigned to human life in the event of safety enhancements, to which my response is an unequivocal no.

The issue often arises from a misunderstanding of the optimized base case. Let's take, for example, the need for a project to construct a new elevated work platform because the current one is compromised and unsafe. Some might argue that there's no financial justification for a new platform when comparing it to the cost of continuing to use the existing unsafe one. However, this comparison is fundamentally flawed because you should not measure the cost-effectiveness of safety upgrades against an unsafe and inadequate status quo. You are not starting with anything close to an optimized base case in these types of situations.

The optimized base case, particularly in the context of safety, must assume we are meeting all necessary safety standards. If the current platform is unsafe, the true base case for comparison isn't the continued use of the unsafe platform but rather the cost of making the existing platform safe. If building a new platform is the only way to achieve the requisite safety standards, then that becomes part of your optimized base case against which other expenses are evaluated.

The core of the problem lies in the identification of viable alternatives. The optimized base case isn't merely about cost-saving; it's fundamentally aligned with our values and principles. When we consider the best outcome achievable without additional spending, it must conform to our core tenet that we do not compromise on safety. Hence, it's clear that using an unsafe platform cannot represent our optimized base case, as it violates our commitment to safety. Having established that the thought of putting anyone at risk is off the table, we must explore the next best solution that requires minimal spending.

> **The optimized base case isn't merely about cost-saving; it's fundamentally aligned with our values and principles.**

If the situation involves accessing an elevated work area, an interim solution might be to rent an aerial lift each time access is required. This necessitates a cost analysis determining how much the rental fees will amount to over a specific period, and how that compares to the expense of constructing a new, safe, and permanent platform. Such a calculation will reveal whether the long-term costs of renting equipment justify the upfront investment in new infrastructure. The optimized base case must reflect the safest, most cost-effective option for the company without compromising our commitment to a harm-free work environment.

Let's take a real-case scenario where a plant required a $50,000 investment to reconstruct the main access road their trucks needed to use when receiving raw materials or preparing outgoing shipments for their customers. The challenge was to demonstrate a positive return on this investment, but the questioning initially led to skepticism. How does simply laying concrete yield financial benefits?

Upon diving into the problem, it became clear that the deteriorating road was causing damage to trucks, creating frustration among suppliers and posing a safety hazard, with the risk of trucks tipping over due to severe potholes. In this context, the optimized base case isn't a "do nothing" approach. Such an option is immediately ruled out for being unsafe and unacceptable. If truck drivers are voicing concerns about hazardous conditions, action must be taken.

We then consider the most feasible non-capital-intensive solution, which could be regularly filling in the potholes with blacktop. Yet this stopgap measure presents its own issues, as these patches are short-lived and require constant reapplication. An evaluation of this temporary fix revealed the ongoing costs to be substantial. Ultimately, this analysis helped illustrate that the upfront capital expenditure for road reconstruction could prove more economical than continuous, less effective maintenance.

This example underscores that the optimized base case should represent the most effective solution that upholds safety standards and mitigates undue costs, even if it involves an initial capital outlay. The recurring costs of temporary patchwork of the potholes, as it turns out, would end up being far costlier than the initial $50,000 investment needed for a new road. This serves to illustrate why establishing an optimized base case is so vital—it becomes the benchmark against which we assess all other alternatives.

**This serves to illustrate why establishing an optimized base case is so vital— it becomes the benchmark against which we assess all other alternatives.**

When it comes to maintenance, capital expenditure, or safety-related investments, the principle is the same. We aim to identify the best method for mitigating risk effectively and efficiently. The optimized base case is predicated on the pursuit of an acceptable and sustainable solution which, in scenarios involving risk, certainly means not continuing with a course of action that perpetuates unacceptable hazards. In practice, such as with the example of remedying a hazardous road, the best course of action aligns with our duty to eliminate risk, maintain safety, and uphold operational integrity. Inherent in this duty is the need to assess long-term costs against immediate investments, ensuring we are not merely deferring expenses but proactively managing our infrastructure.

The scenario is akin to children misusing their sneakers and then requesting new ones. If you have already instructed them to avoid damaging their shoes, especially by playing in the mud, their failure to adhere to those guidelines doesn't automatically qualify them for a new pair. This principle of accountability is COMPARABLE to how we approach project management and maintenance. When applied to the context of business investments or project upkeep, the core message is that preventive measures, care, and prudent use of resources are essential. Just as you expect your kids to take care of their sneakers, we should also expect responsible management in the use of company assets in order to avoid unnecessary expenses. Proper care can prevent premature replacement costs the same way maintaining infrastructure can preclude the need for costly overhauls.

The issue with neglecting equipment maintenance, such as not lubricating machinery, is indeed a common problem in manufacturing. Frequently, there's a request for funds to purchase new machinery under the pretext that the current equipment was not properly maintained. In cases where machinery has deteriorated to the point of being beyond repair despite regular maintenance, the question arises: Is it necessary to buy the latest, most expensive model with additional features? Or is it more practical to replace it with the same model, ensuring that this time around, there will be diligent maintenance?

This presents a decision-making fork in the road where the value of additional features needs to be weighed against the cost. Is investing in the most advanced technology a cost-effective decision that will lead to significant improvements in productivity, or is it an unnecessary expenditure driven by the desire to have the latest features? Ultimately, the goal should not be fixated on acquiring the fanciest option with the newest "bells and whistles." The objective should be to secure equipment that meets the requirements of the production process while ensuring cost-effectiveness and sustainability of the investment through appropriate maintenance.

The lack of a solid maintenance track record undermines confidence in the responsible use of new equipment. Merely replacing machinery without rectifying the underlying maintenance issues does not guarantee a reduction in downtime or cost savings. Rather, it could perpetuate the cycle of neglect and result in more money wasted. You're right to question the logic behind expecting different results with new machinery if the same maintenance practices (or lack thereof) are not addressed. If the previous machine was not maintained, there's a significant risk a new machine would suffer the same fate without a change in maintenance culture.

The more financially sound approach may be to replace the old machine with an identical one, ensuring that maintenance schedules are strictly followed this time. This period should serve as a trial run for establishing responsible maintenance habits. By doing so, not only is money saved on the purchase, but it also fosters a sense of ownership and accountability that should transfer over when the time comes for a future upgrade. And guiding employees to this realization is key—they should buy equipment they can commit to maintaining. Once the new maintenance routines are solidified and proven effective, only then should more expensive options be explored, provided they make sense economically.

## Anchoring Trap

The Anchoring Trap is a potent cognitive bias that subtly influences our decisions. It occurs when people consider a particular value for an unknown quantity before estimating it. This bias can lead us to give disproportionate weight to the first piece of information we receive, setting the stage for potential decision-making pitfalls. The anchoring trap is the reason why we often settle for the first option thrown out at us and can lead to regret after realizing we committed too soon. Think of it like going to a car dealership and looking at the sticker price on a new vehicle. No matter how high that price is, you will likely feel like you got a great deal if the salesperson accepts any offer that is less. The same principle applies if you are selling your car and the buyer starts with an extremely low offer. They likely know you will not accept it, but they have effectively anchored your expectations to a lower number than you expected and set you up to agree to a lower price.

If you want to see just how potent the Anchoring Trap can be in a business situation, try this exercise with your team. Start by dividing everyone up into two groups. Give Group 1 a piece of paper with the following questions:

A. Is the population of Australia more or less than 20 million?
B. What is the population of Australia?

Give Group 2 a piece of paper with the following questions:

A. Is the population of Australia more or less than 75 million?

B. What is the population of Australia?

Collect the answers from both teams and average their responses. You will find that the average estimation by Group 2 is significantly higher than that of Group 1 because the respondents were anchored with a higher suggested population in question B as opposed to question A (75 million versus 20 million). This simple exercise vividly illustrates how the anchoring trap can affect our decision-making processes. It highlights our tendency to anchor our judgments to the initial information we encounter, even when it lacks relevance or accuracy. Because of this, the anchoring trap can impact all areas of our daily lives. Marketers, salespeople, and lawyers are well aware of the anchoring trap's power and frequently use it to manipulate us through advertisements, sales pitches, and negotiations.

However, its impact is not confined to these areas. The anchoring trap can influence virtually every brainstorming activity, hindering our ability to think creatively and generate innovative solutions. Consider your team's brainstorming sessions. The first idea presented often serves as an anchor for the rest of the discussion, limiting the team's creativity and its capacity to explore alternative problem-solving approaches.

> **The anchoring trap can influence virtually every brainstorming activity, hindering our ability to think creatively and generate innovative solutions.**

So, how can you mitigate the Anchoring Trap's influence and empower your team to think more independently and creatively? Start by sharing your carefully framed Opportunity Statement from the first step in the DMF. Refrain from immediately diving into a discussion about capturing the opportunity, instead having each team member take a few minutes to write down their ideas independently. This initial step prevents team members from prematurely anchoring on and being influenced by others' ideas.

Once everyone has their ideas on paper, go around the room and have people share what they've written down. This approach allows for a more open and diverse exchange of ideas, unfettered by the Anchoring Trap's influence. By recognizing and actively addressing the Anchoring Trap, you can foster a more creative, open, and effective decision-making process within your team.

## Halo Effect

The Halo Effect is another commonly used term in business, and one that can be extremely detrimental to the decision-making process. The Halo Effect is the tendency for positive impressions of a person, company, brand, or product in one area to positively or negatively influence one's opinion or feelings about how that same entity performs in other unrelated areas. One example of this in business could be the eloquent and charismatic public speaker who instantly captivates a room full of people being asked to negotiate a multi-million dollar closed-door negotiation with a potential client. The expectation is that their stage presence and communication ability will easily translate into this other discipline and make them successful, even though an entirely different set of skills is needed for the negotiation.

With that in mind, let's look at a fictitious situation where you meet a woman named Joan at a party. You immediately find her to be personable and easy to talk to. Later that night, you find yourself part of a conversation about fundraising for one charitable initiative or another. Everyone is trying to make a list of potential donors who would support the initiative when Joan's name is brought up and you are asked if you think she should be on the list. You, after all, had been speaking with her earlier and struck up a rapport. Do you think Joan will contribute?

If you are sitting there scratching your head, then you are not alone. There is simply not enough information at our disposal to determine whether or not Joan has the means, willingness, or both, to be a potential donor. If you allowed the Halo Effect to dictate your response, then the positive impression she left on you after the party might lead you to believe she approaches everything in such a friendly and supportive manner. But there would be no basis for that assumption, which, in business, can get dangerous quickly.

Now, apply the same halo principle to a business decision. You have a job opening that needs to be filled and two candidates who are equally qualified in terms of education and experience have applied. With nothing else to go other than a list of attributes for each candidate provided by your HR director, which one are you more likely to hire?

Allen: intelligent—industrious—impulsive—critical—stubborn—envious

Ben: envious—stubborn—critical—impulsive—industrious—intelligent

It might have taken you a second to realize that both candidates have the exact same attributes, just listed in the opposite order. Allen's qualities are shown from most admirable to least, while Ben's are listed from least desirable to most. Because of the Halo Effect, it is likely many people would have stopped even considering Ben for the job by the time they got to the second or third attribute. But the catch is, no one said these were listed in any particular order. Just because Allen's first adjective was "intelligent" does not mean that is more dominant than his "envious" trait that is listed last. We just created that halo for him in our own minds.

One of the best ways to avoid falling victim to the Halo Effect, or allowing your people to do so if you are the leader, is a two-part fix. The first is to allow everyone involved in the discussion to write all their ideas down on a piece of paper before allowing anyone to begin sharing. This way people won't censor their answers because someone else already said something similar to what they were thinking. Tying in with this lack of censorship would also be to ensure the leaders let everyone else in the room share their ideas and discuss them before making their own suggestions and avoid the instinctive reaction for everyone to smile and nod at those in charge.

## Status-quo Trap

We are biased toward maintaining the current situation, even when a better alternative exists. The rationale behind this offers great insight into many areas of our lives. Too many people stay in unhealthy relationships solely because they have always (or as far back as they can remember) been with that person. We will avoid asking our boss for a raise for fear that he may also ask for something in return from us, thus disrupting the status quo. This can come into play during even the most basic of situations like sticking through a bad movie because those you went with are still in their seats. It is easier to do nothing than to run the risk of causing a disruption, even if it turns out to be a positive one.

To see an example of this in real life, let's look at an instance where two neighboring states, New Jersey and Pennsylvania, made similar changes in their laws to reduce insurance costs. Each state gave drivers a new option: by accepting a limited right to sue, they could lower their premiums. But the two states framed the choice in very different ways. In New Jersey, you automatically got the limited right to sue unless you specified otherwise. In Pennsylvania, you got the full right to sue unless you specified otherwise. The different frames established a different status quo in each state, and, not surprisingly, most consumers defaulted to the status quo. As a result, in New Jersey about 80% of drivers chose the limited right to sue, but in Pennsylvania only 25% chose it. Because of the way it framed the choice, Pennsylvania failed to gain approximately $200 million in expected insurance and litigation savings.

As a business example that most people who have ever worked in the corporate world can relate to, think about what happens when you are first given the option for enrolling in the benefits package. If a 401k is an option, the enrollment rate is directly impacted by whether or not the default option is for the participant to be enrolled automatically or for them to manually enroll. If a company wants to increase their participation numbers, all they need to do is make automatic enrollment the default option and most will never opt out of it. The opposite is true when the participants must enroll, negatively impacting enrollment rates. For a truly unbiased decision from the participants, the company should explore an enrollment option where the participant must select either a yes or no, with no default option available to quickly bypass the decision-making process.

It may not be easy to choose action over remaining the same, but it can be done. Always remind yourself of your objectives, then examine how they would be served by the status quo. After a careful and unbiased review, you may find that elements of the current situation act as barriers to your goals. While the status quo can be seen as your only alternative, since it is already in place, it can just as easily be the biggest roadblock to progress in other areas. Identify other options and use them as counterbalances, carefully evaluating all the pluses and minuses. Here are some best practices I have used throughout my own career and consulting practice to put the bigger picture in perspective:

- Ask yourself whether you would choose the status-quo alternative if, in fact, it weren't the status quo.
- Avoid exaggerating the effort or cost involved in switching from the status quo.
- Remember that the desirability of the status quo will change over time. When comparing alternatives, always evaluate them in terms of the future as well as the present.
- If you have several alternatives that are superior to the status quo, don't default to the status quo just because you're having a hard time picking the best alternative. Force yourself to choose.

## Best Practices to Incorporate

Visit www.enablingempowerment.com to download these tools
- Brainstorming Tip Sheet
- Optimized Base Case Tip Sheet

6

# Step 3 - Identify Key Drivers

**NOW THAT WE** have developed a list of creative alternatives and narrowed it down to a few that are most viable, it is time to really see how they stack up against each other. While they may all seem like good choices, after all they did make it past the initial cut, chances are your organization has limited resources and as such can only act on the best of the bunch. For there to be alignment here, we need to think back to Step 1, where we defined the opportunity statement. No matter how great a solution may seem, it has to solve the issue at hand.

If your goal was to improve adjusted gross margin, the only ideas that matter at this stage are ones with a direct impact on that goal. That's not to say a solution that might reduce workplace injuries by 25% is not a noble idea or something that can't be explored at a later date when solving for a different issue, just that it is irrelevant to improving the margin.

One of the best ways I have found to accomplish this is by creating a cause-effect map to help identify the second and third order effects. Having various layers and sequences of events that impact a final cause laid out on paper forces System 2 to engage and bypass the System 1 response of accepting any idea that increases revenue or reduces cost to be the most fitting. You can find an example of such a map as it relates to this example when we get to the Decision Trap for Base-Rate Neglect.

---

Before we dive deeper into differentiating between which key drivers will be the most impactful, it is first important to ask the right questions that can help identify the potential key drivers we have to choose from:

- What are all the elements that drive the profitability of this venture?
- What will make the venture successful?
- What will make the venture unsuccessful?
- What is the basic range of outcomes for each driver (historical, industry trend, POV, gut feel)?
- Which drivers have the biggest impact on profitability?
- What are all the assumptions you are making?
- Have you found/sought the best knowledge?

Sensitivity analysis is a great tool for separating one great idea from another. At face value, multiple key drivers identified through the process above could appear equally beneficial, making it difficult to decide which one to implement. Sensitivity analysis helps decision-makers dive deeper by determining how different values of an independent variable affect a particular dependent variable under a given set of assumptions. Plainly translated, sensitivity analyses study how various sources of uncertainty in a mathematical model contribute to the model's overall uncertainty. This technique is used within specific boundaries that depend on one or more input variables.

The underlying belief with sensitivity analysis is that not all variables will have the same degree of effect on an outcome when evaluated proportionately. As we will see in the chart displayed in Base-Rate Neglect, two variables can have significantly different impacts on an outcome. When applied to the same degree, Variable A and Variable B could both potentially increase a result by 10%. However, if the attention or weighting given to those variables increased, the outputs might not correlate exactly. Let's say you double the efforts for both variables A and B. It would be natural to think that this should result in a 20% increase in sales across the board. But depending on the underlying sensitivity of the options, one might find that Option A is rigid and still only offers a 10% increase despite the extra effort or resources, while Option B yields a 30% increase. Once compared in that light, depending on the scale to which you wish to focus, Option B can quickly look like the better choice.

In addition to sensitivity analysis, we can also use the 80/20 Rule, commonly known as the Pareto Principle, to analyze key drivers in a different way. The 80/20 Rule stipulates that 80% of the outcome usually depends on 20% of the Key Drivers. After you have conducted a sensitivity analysis, identify those few Key Drivers that can genuinely make or break your decision. This simplifies your efforts as you move into Step 4 of the DMF, "Manage the Risks and Upsides." Understanding the hidden factors that drive decision-making can significantly enhance the quality of your choices. By recognizing Decision Traps like Base- Rate Neglect and applying tools and tips to identify Key Drivers, you can navigate the complex landscape of decisions with greater precision and confidence. So, the next time you're faced with a tough choice, remember: it's not just about the obvious details but also the hidden ones that truly matter.

It can be easy to fall victim to thinking that all potential variables in your decision-making landscape carry equal

**It can be easy to fall victim to thinking that all potential variables in your decision-making landscape carry equal weight, but that is just not true.**

weight, but that is just not true. In any given situation you could have dozens of potential variables to consider, but only a handful of them will truly be good or bad. Most are inconsequential and not be worth the investment of time or resources to pursue beyond the identification phase. Using the 80/20 Rule in conjunction with a thorough sensitivity analysis will ensure that only the most impactful key drivers make it through to the final decision-making process, thus making you more operationally and fiscally efficient.

## Base-Rate Neglect

Base-Rate Neglect can be a widespread decision-making oversight. The phenomenon occurs primarily because, in the absence of explicit statistical information provided within a given problem, our brain is predisposed to conclude such statistics are non-existent. If the brain is not provided with the base rate statistics as part of the problem or question being solved, it assumes no such data exists. This is a simplified assumption System One employs as part of the earlier concept where we learned about "what you see is all there is." The system operates on the logic that it must rapidly render decisions based solely on the information that is currently available, without a search for additional context. In this automatic mode, the brain does not pause to reflect on the possibility that there could be underlying statistics or base rates which are important to forming a more accurate judgment.

By understanding this, we can demonstrate how the brain's instinctual reliance on the immediately visible information leads to a negligence of foundational data, which in turn can skew decision-making processes and lead to potentially flawed conclusions. In the scenario we are about to cover, we are not provided with base rate statistics that compare the number of salespeople to librarians. Therefore, your brain will not factor in those statistics. The only details given describe Ronald as meek and introverted. Consequently, our brain tends to assume the information presented is the complete set needed for answering a question that should require more information if we are to be accurate.

Consider a scenario where you must decide if a gentleman named Ronald is either a librarian or a salesman. His personality can best be described as retiring. There is no doubt that he is an introvert. If you had nothing else to go on other than those two attributes, which do you think Ronald is more likely to be? At first glance, most of us might assume Ronald leans toward being a librarian. After all, many salespeople are known for their outgoing and gregarious nature, seemingly incompatible with introversion. But before we lock ourselves into a decision, let's add some more context. There are approximately 150,000 librarians in the US. Not a small number at first glance, but compare that to the staggering 5,800,000 salespeople in the US.

This information should give us pause, bypassing System 1 and the easier answer it came up with at face value. If System 2 is allowed to weigh in and run some calculations, the answer no longer seems so clear. Even if only three out of every 100 salespeople are introverts, there are more introverted salespeople than librarians. Did you consider this statistical fact before forming your initial opinion? Chances are, like most people, you did not. This is a classic example of Base-Rate Neglect, where we focus on specific information while ignoring broader statistical data.

As Daniel Kahneman eloquently states in his book *Thinking, Fast and Slow,* "The confidence that individuals have in their beliefs depends mostly on the quality of the story they can tell about what they see, even if they see little. We often fail to allow for the possibility that evidence that should be critical to our judgment is missing."

> **The confidence that individuals have in their beliefs depends mostly on the quality of the story they can tell about what they see, even if they see little.**

But how does this affect decision-making in our everyday lives? In the DMF, Step 2 involves identifying creative alternatives, while our current Step 3 involves pinpointing the Key Drivers that can determine the success or failure of each alternative. Awareness of our tendency to neglect base-rate data is crucial, as it can lead us to overlook essential information that aids us in estimating the likelihood of success or failure. We already know our brains often gloss over statistical information and favor correlation over causation.

To circumvent this Decision Trap, consider creating a cause map such as the one we discussed earlier for each alternative you're exploring. A cause map visually illustrates the cause-and-effect relationships involved, helping your team identify all variables that may affect the decision's outcome. An example of a cause map that could be used to determine what solutions would be most impactful when determining how to improve adjusted gross margin might look something like the diagram below.

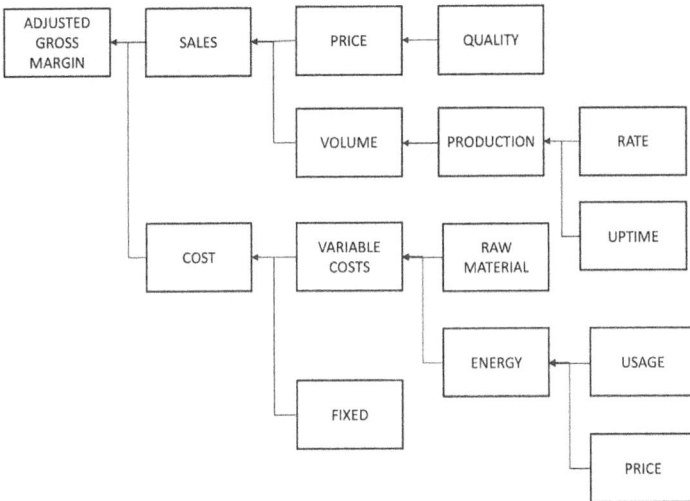

The utilization of sensitivity analysis when dealing with areas of uncertainty is another way to overcome Base-Rate Neglect. Sometimes, we must make decisions in the face of uncertainty about base-rate data. Here, sensitivity analysis becomes invaluable. It helps us gauge the impact of a change in a Key Driver on the overall decision outcome. By analyzing sensitivity graphs, you can prioritize your analysis efforts effectively. For instance, in the sensitivity graphs below, we can see that a 1% change in the incremental margin affects the project's expected Net Present Value (NPV) by >$17MM. In comparison, a 1% change in electric expense only has a $300K impact on NPV. Based on that information, we need to spend much more time understanding what can change the incremental margin than we spend analyzing the electric expense.

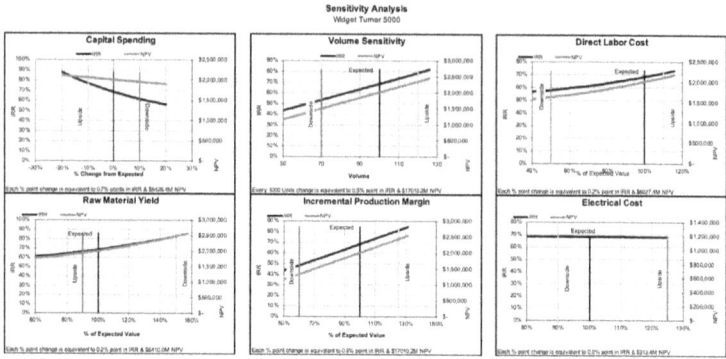

Sensitivity Analysis
Widget Turner 5000

# Representativeness

Representativeness occurs when an individual erroneously believes a certain random event is less likely or more likely to happen based on the outcome of a previous event or series of events. To best illustrate this concept, consider the four rows of numbers below. Two were generated by a random number generator, and two were generated by a human. Can you tell which two were generated by a human?

11000111111001001001
11000001010101010100000
10101110101000111010
001100011010000111011

The answer is that the last two rows were generated by a human. What you will notice is that the first two rows, which were generated by a truly random number generator, have strings of five or more "1's" or "0's." Even though we know that the appearance of either a 1 or a 0 as the next number in the sequence is completely independent of whether or not the previous number was a 1 or 0, it is hard for us to believe there could be a fifth after seeing four 1's or 0's in a row.

The same thing happens in almost every instance of a random outcome between two options. When flipping a coin multiple times, we base our next guess, often subconsciously, on the prior outcomes. If we flip three "tails" in a row, we think a "heads" has to be due on one of the next flips. But that isn't the case. The chance of another "tails" is still 50/50. The same thing happens at a roulette wheel in the casino. When you look at the results board for the last few spins and see that "red" has come out four times in a row, it is natural to want to place a bet on "black" because we can't envision a fifth red in a row. This Representativeness Trap affects our decision-making when we look at past events and think we are "due" to get a particular result or outcome.

## Availability Bias

Availability Bias, also known as recallability, is significant because it contributes to numerous decision traps. Availability Bias is closely related to the concept of anchoring. Essentially, it refers to the human tendency to easily remember and give more importance to recent information or events compared to those that happened in the past. This bias means that newer information is often retrieved more quickly and is given disproportionate weight in the decision-making process.

For instance, people often become more concerned about the safety of flying immediately following a reported airplane crash. Once the media begins publicizing what happened, what the possible causes were, and how many people died as a result of the crash, there is often a marked increase in aviation safety concerns among the general public. This heightened concern is not necessarily reflective of the actual risks of flying, which remain statistically low, but it illustrates the impact of recent events on our psyche. Because the crash is fresh in people's minds, they place more emphasis on it and may overestimate the dangers of flying, which is actually safer than driving a car or riding a bicycle in a major city.

In the wake of a significant earthquake, there is an identifiable spike in public anxiety about the occurrence of another similar event. This heightened state of concern is, in part, a result of availability bias, where recent events loom larger in our perception than they perhaps should when assessing risks rationally. This bias can skew our understanding of what is truly dangerous. Moreover, when considering different types of tragedies, people are generally more fearful of rare but catastrophic events, like that large earthquake, compared to more mundane, yet statistically deadlier risks, such as car accidents. This fear is exacerbated by media coverage, which tends to spotlight the extraordinary over the commonplace; a massive earthquake will dominate news cycles, while the daily incidents of rush hour traffic accidents receive far less attention despite their greater frequency.

The phenomenon of Availability Bias means you are more likely to vividly remember dramatic or horrific events, such as murders, which can disproportionately influence your fears of something similar happening to you. Consequently, you might find yourself more afraid of being attacked by someone in a parking lot than facing the hazards of rush-hour driving, despite the higher statistical probability of an accident occurring on the road.

This bias messes with our perception of risk; we tend to overestimate the likelihood of events that are easily recalled and underestimate those that we don't think about as often, regardless of their actual chances of happening. Availability Bias can contribute to the Anchoring Trap in Step 2 of the DMF because once a specific piece of information is established in your mind—such as a number or a recent event—it becomes a mental reference point that is easily recalled during decision-making. This is particularly relevant when estimating the likelihood of a project or idea's success. If you have recently been involved in a successful project similar to the one you're considering, you are more likely to believe the new project will also succeed. This optimistic forecast may not be supported by the underlying statistics, which could suggest a different outcome, but the recent success messes with your judgment because it is more readily available in your memory.

> We tend to overestimate the likelihood of events that are easily recalled and underestimate those that we don't think about as often, regardless of their actual chances of happening.

## Best Practices to Incorporate

Visit www.enablingempowerment.com to download these tools
- Business Driver Cause-Effect Map
- Sensitivity Analysis
- 80/20 Rule

# 7

# Step 4 - Manage Risk and Upside

**HAVE YOU EVER** presented a meticulously crafted forecast, only to be met with a skeptical eyebrow raised at the precise decimal point? Of course, what comes next is a debate over minutiae that really have little impact on the final decision. That's the Overconfidence Trap in action, and it's one we all fall into. But what if, instead of fixating on a single point, we embraced the inherent uncertainty of the future and explored a range of possibilities? After all, none of us have a crystal ball and the likelihood of a decision not working out the way we hoped is bound to happen at least once, if not dozens of times throughout our careers and lives.

My encounter with this shift in perspective came during a presentation for a new technology investment. My financial analysis boasted an expected savings of $1,651,487.73. The CFO looked me straight in the eye and asked, "Sure about that 73 cents?"

His question struck a chord. My spreadsheet might have spat out that precise figure, but did I truly believe it down to the penny? Of course not. Yet, presenting it as such implied an unfounded level of certainty. That's when he introduced me to the power of ranges. Instead of fixating on a single point estimate, the CFO suggested exploring a range of potential outcomes, each with its own probability. This reframed the discussion. Suddenly, the focus shifted from debating individual cents to understanding the broader landscape of possibilities. Now, instead of debating minutiae, we could explore the really important questions like:

- How confident are we that the worst-case scenario won't be even worse?

- What factors could push results toward the lower or higher end of the range, and how can we manage them?
- What does the size of the range tell us about our overall confidence, and how can we narrow it down?

This wasn't just about making better predictions; it was about making better decisions. As Daniel Kahneman, the Nobel laureate, aptly put it, "Overconfidence is the most significant single obstacle to the improvement of human

> **"Overconfidence is the most significant single obstacle to the improvement of human decisions."**

decisions." This is where this 4th step of the process we are now discussing directly tackles the Overconfidence Trap by encouraging us to identify our 90% Confidence Interval for each key decision driver. This is precisely what makes my DMF different from what just about every company out there is teaching. Imagine a table like this:

EXAMPLE: KEY DRIVERS AND RANGE OF OUTCOMES

| KEY DRIVER | EXPECTED | UPSIDE | DOWNSIDE | ASSUMPTIONS |
|---|---|---|---|---|
| INCREMENTAL PRODUCTION | 100K/day | 200K/day | 50K/day | Expected: Production increase of 4tph based on experimental data<br>Up: Production increase of 8tph based on manufacturer's claims<br>Down: Reduced raw material supply limits production |
| RAW MATERIAL COST SAVINGS | $1/TON | $5/TON | $-1/TON | Expected: Assumes 2% improvement in yield based on experiment and current raw material costs<br>Up: Yield improves 10% per manufacturer<br>Down: Raw material costs increase due to production increase and higher marginal cost |
| TOOLING LIFE | 1,000 HRS/DIE | 1,000 HRS/DIE | 800 HRS/DIE | Expected: Based on experimental data using 3 "test dies"<br>Upside: Unlikely to be better than the experiment<br>Down: Increased production rates cause faster die wear |

Such a table not only sparks productive discussions about potential risks and upsides but also serves as a valuable documentation tool. When revisiting the decision later, we can avoid the "Hindsight Trap" and clearly recall the assumptions we made. Embracing ranges doesn't negate the importance of thorough analysis; it simply adds a layer of realism and flexibility. It's about acknowledging the inherent uncertainty of the future while still making informed choices. So, the next time you find yourself presenting a forecast, remember that the only thing you know for sure is that your single-point estimate is wrong. Instead, unlock the power of ranges and watch your decisions soar beyond the confines of overconfidence.

**The next time you find yourself presenting a forecast, remember that the only thing you know for sure is that your single-point estimate is wrong.**

Another way of managing risks is through the power of people both outside your organization and within. The outside view, where we bring in paid consultants, can be a powerful perspective since they do not have any of the potential biases that those close to the process may have. If you want to increase your factory output by 20%, it might take more than just your plant manager's willingness and ability to ramp up production to that level even if your machines have the capacity. The outside view can take into account factors such as:

- Suppliers: Do the companies who supply your raw material have the capacity to increase your order size to meet new targets?

- Supply chain: Does the industry have the ability to meet the needs of your suppliers on a continuous basis?
- Economics: Will prices and interest rates remain stable so that your current budgeting forecasts for the increased raw materials will remain sufficient?

While all this data can be priceless in many ways, not all organizations will find themselves in a place where they can afford to pay for private consultants. In those instances, our own employees can serve in a similar capacity when we leverage the practice of red teaming, a military term for tasking someone with poking holes in our theory or belief.

Using the same example above, you might consider forming two teams of employees, giving one the focus of strictly focusing on all the reasons this endeavor will be successful and the other on only poking holes and playing devil's advocate. With the data gathered from the two very different points of view, management can then draw from best case and worst case scenarios to revise their projections if needed.

## Law of Small Numbers

This is a bias where people tend to draw broad conclusions from small data sets. This arises partly because our brains are not naturally inclined toward statistical thinking or complex mathematical concepts. Consequently, we often overvalue the significance of information derived from a small sample size and underestimate the potential for such limited data to mislead us. The law of small numbers can be seen as the opposite of the law of large numbers, which states that as a sample size increases, the sample mean will more closely approximate the population mean. Conversely, a smaller sample size is more prone to deviations from the population average.

For instance, consider two hospitals: one that delivers ten thousand babies in a year, and another that delivers a thousand. The hospital with fewer deliveries (a thousand babies) is more likely to experience greater fluctuations in the daily ratio of boys to girls born. This is because a smaller sample size offers greater scope for variability and less statistical stability than a larger one. The common perception is that the chances of a baby being a boy or a girl are evenly split at fifty-fifty, leading to the expectation that a hospital would have an equal number of boy and girl births over time, regardless of the number of babies delivered. However, this isn't exactly the case when we consider fluctuations that can occur within smaller samples.

In a smaller hospital that delivers a thousand babies annually, a slight increase in the birth of boys over girls, even just on a few days, can significantly affect the overall ratio. This is because each single event has a larger impact on the total average due to the smaller sample size. On the other hand, in a larger hospital with ten thousand deliveries a year, the same small variances from day to day are less likely to influence the overall gender ratio noticeably. This larger sample size tends to even out short-term fluctuations due to the law of large numbers, making the birth ratio appear closer to the expected fifty-fifty split over time. To break it down even further, imagine a hospital where two babies are born. The likelihood of both being boys or girls is significantly higher than with a hundred or a thousand.

To use a different example for frame of reference, let's look at baseball. Whether we realize it or not, most of us have quoted a baseball analogy when we say some is "batting 1,000." It can be used sarcastically or genuinely, but the base meaning is that someone is on a roll—their results have been perfect. And while that is true, anyone who has ever followed baseball knows that there is a big difference between a batter with a 100% batting average who has only been up to the plate once and someone who is batting .333 but has been up to the plate a thousand times. The batter with one plate appearance will be batting .250 if they get out on their next three appearances while the batter with a thousand appearances will only see their average drop to .332 if they get out the next three at bats. Sample size matters—a lot!

**Sample size matters—a lot! Evaluating the success of a decision based on a small sample size can lead to misleading conclusions because it may not truly represent what would happen in a larger population.**

Evaluating the success of a decision based on a small sample size can lead to misleading conclusions because it may not truly represent what would happen in a larger population. Take, for example, a company that installs a new machine. If a manager looks at only three instances of installation to deduce the average production output, they are basing their judgment on an insufficient number of cases. It's quite risky to assume the fourth installation of a machine will produce similar results to those previously observed. A better approach would be to ask, "How many times has this machine been installed industry-wide?"

This small dataset doesn't account for the range of potential outcomes and the different factors that could influence the machine's performance in various scenarios. For a more accurate assessment, it would require looking at a larger number of installations over time and across different contexts to understand the average production levels, identify any trends, and make allowances for anomalies. Doing so would provide a more comprehensive view of the machine's performance and a better foundation for decision-making.

Relating this to baseball statistics offers a clear example. If a player gets up to bat four times and strikes out each time, their batting average is zero. But it's crucial to note that this statistic is based on a very limited number of at-bats. Yes, striking out every time indicates poor performance, but this player only needs to get one hit to now be batting .200, and with two hits they would have an outstanding .333 batting average. This is precisely why drawing conclusions from such a scant number of at-bats can be misleading. Whether batting zero or .333, we do not have a large enough sample size to determine if this player is good at the plate or not.

Indeed, placing too much emphasis on a player's performance over the past week rather than considering their entire career record is where the error lies. It's a common fallacy to overvalue short-term results. A player might have a bad week, but career statistics could indicate that they are, in fact, a **It's a common fallacy to overvalue short-term results.** much better hitter. Therefore, it's crucial to avoid overemphasizing small sample sizes and to look at the larger, more representative set of data to gauge true ability or performance. This principle can be applied exactly the same way to how we evaluate the performance of an employee, a process, or a production line.

## Overconfidence

Even though most of us are not very good at making estimates or forecasts, we actually tend to be overconfident about our accuracy. A lot of people push back on that claim, so I created an exercise for participants to illustrate just how true it is. The activity includes ten questions designed to demonstrate exactly this point to the participants. Some of the questions might include: "How old was Martin Luther King Jr. when he died?" or "What is the average gestation period of an African elephant?" or even "What is the distance to the moon in miles?" Participants are then instructed to provide a range of answers for each question in which they are 90% confident contains the actual answer. The purpose of this exercise is to challenge assumptions and illustrate the concept of uncertainty within estimates.

If you excel at the estimation exercise, the expected result would be that you accurately include the correct answer within your estimated ranges for nine out of the ten questions, since you are aiming for a 90% confidence level. However, when this exercise is conducted in large groups, it's often observed that participants typically only manage to get about four or five questions right, meaning that for just about half of the questions, their estimated ranges actually encompass the true answers. This discrepancy highlights a common overconfidence in our ability to estimate and predict outcomes accurately.

Our tendency to be overconfident often leads to underestimating the scope of what we don't know. Therefore, in an exercise like this, choosing an extremely broad range—for example, from zero to infinity—for all ten questions might yield a more accurate outcome, ensuring that the true answers fall within the estimated ranges. While choosing such broad ranges is not the ideal strategy for precision, it ironically might result in a perfect score, with the true answers falling within all ten of the provided ranges, compared to the commonly observed score of only four or five correct answers out of ten. This outcome serves as a reminder that we often overestimate the accuracy of our knowledge and predictions.

This tendency toward overconfidence is particularly prevalent when dealing with the unknown, such as projecting future sales or anticipating the price of a commodity five years from now. Often, we overestimate our ability to predict these figures accurately. That's why employing strategies such as a premortem can be valuable. This technique involves a proactive stance where, for instance, you would critique a project by examining the potential reasons for its failure ahead of time. So if someone projects that a project will generate between five and ten million dollars a year, conducting a premortem would help in assessing the confidence levels of these estimates and identifying factors that could lead to different outcomes.

Envision this scenario: it is a year from now, and instead of making a profit of five to ten million dollars, we have incurred a loss of five million dollars. I want you to construct a narrative around this outcome. What transpired over the year to lead to such a loss? By asking you to recount this hypothetical scenario, it encourages the team to think creatively and consider a range of possibilities outside their usual expectations. Although it might be challenging to conceive such scenarios, this exercise is often effective in revealing overlooked risks or unforeseen events. Team members might realize potential pitfalls that had not been previously considered. This method effectively stretches our understanding of what could happen, broadening the perceived range of possible outcomes and preparing us better for uncertainty.

## Confirmation Bias

Confirmation Bias simply states that humans tend to seek information that confirms our hypothesis and ignore information that disproves it. Instead of objectively and impartially analyzing data to build a case for or against something, we will cherry pick the information that supports the outcome we desire. Imagine the age old debate of whether dogs or cats make a better pet. Dog lovers will undoubtedly find all the research that supports the claim for dogs while cat lovers will overlook all that information in favor of what they find that supports a cat as the superior house pet.

This bias starts from the moment you begin the research process. Just think for a second about how you frame your online searches. To try getting impartial search results, the proper question to search in this scenario would be something along the lines of "Do dogs or cats make better pets?" Instead, what most biased searches will read is more along the lines of "Are dogs better than cats?" from which the top results will typically list various reasons supporting the idea that dogs are the superior pet. These articles cater to the viewpoint implied by the search query.

However, if you change your search to "Why cats are better than dogs," you will find a completely different set of articles, ones that will provide arguments in favor of cats. This illustrates how the information we encounter can be skewed by the nature of our inquiries, reinforcing our preconceptions and highlighting the ease with which we can find supporting evidence for either side of an argument in the digital age.

Our inherent biases often shape the way we seek out information. For instance, if one starts with the belief that dogs are the preferable pet, confirmation bias may lead them to search specifically for "Why are dogs better than cats?" The search results of this query

**Our inherent biases often shape the way we seek out information.**

will likely reinforce this dog-centric view, presenting articles and arguments that support the superiority of dogs. This underscores a crucial aspect of information search behavior: the formulation of a query can direct us either toward confirmation of our existing opinions or toward a broader spectrum of knowledge. It is essential to be mindful of the biases inherent in our questions to ensure that we are not simply validating our beliefs but exploring a topic more thoroughly.

## Best Practices to Incorporate

Visit www.enablingempowerment.com to download these tools
- Key Driver Upside/Downside Table
- Premortem Tip Sheet
- Outside View/Red Teaming

# 8

# Step 5 - Perform Economic Analysis

**ECONOMIC ANALYSIS IS,** or at least should be, the basis for all decisions in business. Unless you are running a non-profit, and even then money is vital to keeping the doors open, maximizing the returns on any given investment is crucial to long term success. No one goes into business to sell their products or services at a loss, and not paying attention to the potential returns, or losses, on investments is no different. And while there are many different ways to calculate ROI, we at Enabling Empowerment have created a proprietary model that can be used in almost all use cases. As a disclaimer, this single chapter will not be enough to teach all the economic principles your team should have an understanding of. That could be an entire series of books given the college level coursework available on the topics, which underscores why every organization should be offering courses and training for employee development in these areas.

Our financial model aligns with the Enabling Empowerment approach, allowing you to evaluate a range of outcomes and scenarios. It provides a holistic view of your project's potential, enabling you to identify risks and opportunities in a simplified manner. You don't need to be an expert in tax accounting or finance to navigate complex financial calculations. Our model does the heavy lifting, saving you time and effort. And it does this by looking beyond standard metrics like Net Present Value (NPV), Internal Rate of Return (IRR), and Earnings Before Interest, Taxes, Depreciation, and Amortization (EBITDA), to account for the sensitivity analysis we learned about in Chapter 6. This powerful feature helps you understand the key drivers of risk and upside to your investment, enabling more informed decision-making.

There are numerous benefits to using our financial model not always found in many of the other options you might currently be using. The first and most notable ties in with the premise of this entire book, which is to create a streamlined decision-making process. Our model simplifies and streamlines the decision-making process, allowing you to evaluate the financial viability of your capital project efficiently. With automated calculations and built-in formulas, our financial model eliminates the need for manual calculations, offering the added benefit of saving you valuable time and effort. And last but not least, the model will help you gain a comprehensive understanding of the risks and benefits associated with your specific project.

Our model provides insights into various scenarios, empowering you to make well-informed decisions. Using graphic representation so the data you enter makes visualizing complex financial data more easily digestible. These visuals enhance your ability to communicate the basis of your recommendations to decision-makers effectively, bolstering your credibility as someone who has taken the time to fully understand the complex variables at play.

While our financial model is available for anyone to use no matter what level of financial analysis experience you have, there are still some prerequisites to keep in mind before plugging in data. A basic understanding of Excel is recommended to leverage our financial model's full potential. Familiarity with spreadsheet functions and formulas will enable you to navigate and customize the model to suit your specific project requirements. The calculations performed in this comprehensive financial modeling program combined with a sophisticated user-friendly interface will empower you with accurate data, insights, and a streamlined decision-making process. Invest in your success today!

## Sunk Costs

The term sunk, as it relates to sunk cost, is derived from the belief that any investment already "sunk" into a prior decision can justify sticking by those prior choices even when they no longer seem valid. Think of it in terms of the expression "throwing good money after bad," which symbolizes the refusal to admit a decision did not work out as planned. And, as often happens in this type of situation, we just keep sinking more money into the prior mistake under the false belief that eventually we can turn it around. Well, I am here to tell you that it does not work that way.

Take, for example, purchasing a non-refundable, non-transferable ticket to a concert or event; the money spent on this ticket is considered '"sunk" because the purchaser has no other recourse for the money they spent other than attend the event. On the other hand, the sunk cost fallacy arises from a misjudgment—specifically, not taking sunk costs into account appropriately when deciding future actions.

Consider what happens when the evening of the concert arrives, and you find yourself feeling under the weather. Ignoring the principles of sunk cost fallacy, you might argue, "Since I've already spent the money, I should go, regardless of the fact that I'm feeling ill and would genuinely prefer to stay at home." This line of thinking overlooks that the money spent is already "sunk" and non-recoverable; attending the concert does not change that fact. Therefore, the logical approach would be to make a decision based on your current state of well-being, not the expenditure from the past, which would likely lead to choosing comfort over fulfilling a sense of obligation to use the ticket.

In addition, attending the concert will not only be about dealing with discomfort—it will incur additional expenses as well. You will find yourself having to spend more on transportation, parking, and possibly purchasing food while you are out. This is all to engage in an activity you are not keen on because you are not feeling well, driven by the feeling of obligation stemming from the initial monetary outlay. It is an adherence to the fallacy that because money has been spent on the ticket, you must follow through to justify that expense, regardless of accruing further costs and regardless of your lack of enthusiasm for the event. Wise decision-making would suggest reassessing whether the pursuit of sunk costs with further investment truly enhances your well-being or if it would be better to simply write off the money spent and move on.

The Sunk Cost Fallacy, or Sunk Cost Trap as it is sometimes referred to, poses a significant risk in the business environment. It can prompt managers and entrepreneurs to throw that proverbial good money after the bad just to avoid admitting the initial decision did not work out as planned. This happens when individuals continue investing in a failing project simply because they have already invested a substantial amount. The initial investment exerts an undue influence on their decisions, leading them to overlook the likelihood of diminishing returns.

Suppose a company has invested in a piece of machinery, which subsequently underperforms and fails to meet production expectations. Even when it becomes apparent that the machine will not yield the projected output, there may be a reluctance to invest further. The concern is that any additional funds will only marginally improve the machine's performance, not enough to meet the initial targets, but leaders might continue funding improvements due to the amount already spent. A rational approach would require evaluating whether further investments could ever deliver an acceptable return, irrespective of previous expenditures.

In essence, the Sunk Cost Fallacy can blindside business decision-making, leading to continued investment in unprofitable ventures and impeding the identification of more lucrative opportunities. It is crucial to focus on future benefits and feasibility rather than past costs to avoid this pitfall. Although the initial investment in whatever the initiative might have been is no longer recoverable, a modest additional outlay may still be worthwhile. Despite the machine not meeting initial expectations, investing a bit more could yield a net positive return on this subsequent expense. Differentiating between unrecoverable past costs and potential future gains is crucial. It is the prospective incremental benefit that is key to informing whether further financial commitment makes sense.

> **The Sunk Cost Fallacy can blindside business decision-making, leading to continued investment in unprofitable ventures and impeding the identification of more lucrative opportunities.**

The nice thing about the sunk cost decision trap is that it is easily avoided once you are aware it is happening. Seek out and listen carefully to the views of people who were uninvolved with the earlier decisions and who are hence unlikely to be committed to them. Leveraging unbiased parties who have no vested interest in proving a bad decision was a good one for the sake of their own egos can help level the playing field when approaching those who made the original decision. It can be easier to get buy-in around changing a course of action when it feels like a collaborative effort and not an "I told you so" type of conversation.

If you are at the root of the decision gone wrong, examine why admitting to an earlier mistake distresses you. If the problem lies in your own wounded self-esteem, deal with it head-on. Remind yourself that even smart choices can have bad consequences through no fault of the original decision-maker, and that even the best and most experienced managers are not immune to errors in judgment. Remember the wise words of Warren Buffet: "When you find yourself in a hole, the best thing you can do is stop digging."

> **"When you find yourself in a hole, the best thing you can do is stop digging."**

Be on the lookout for the influence of sunk-cost biases in the decisions and recommendations made by your subordinates. Reassign responsibilities when necessary to shake up the thought process. But at the same time, don't cultivate a failure-fearing culture that leads employees to perpetuate their mistakes. In rewarding people, look at the quality of their decision-making (taking into account what was known at the time their decisions were made), not just the quality of the outcomes.

## Time Value of Money

The time value of money is a key component of any college finance or economics program. In basic English, the concept states that at any given point in time a certain amount of money may be worth more or less than face value. This does not necessarily mean that a hundred dollar bill will have a face value of more or less than one hundred tomorrow, next week, or a year in the future. But what it does state is that based on the underlying need or use case, the perceived value of that hundred dollars to an end user can be drastically different.

Let's say I offered you $1,000 today, or $1,000 a year from now. Which one would you take? Like most people, you would probably prefer to have the money right now since there is no added benefit to waiting a year for the same amount of money. If we change the example to offering the choice between $900 today or $1,000 a year from now, we probably have more people considering holding out to make an extra hundred dollars. There might even be situations where someone would be willing to pay me $5, $10, or more to secure the $1,000 today because of that opportunity cost we spoke about back in Step 1.

That is the whole concept of interest. The situation arises when people fail to properly account for the reduced value of future money compared to today's money in their financial analysis. When this factor is not considered, there is a risk of overvaluing a project. It is important to integrate appropriate financial measures, such as discounted cash flow analysis, to accurately assess a project's worth by understanding the present value of future cash flows. Going back to the examples

I just gave, let's look at two simple situations involving Tim and Mary where they are both given three choices:

Choice A: Receive $1,000 today, but return $200 of it within twelve months.

Choice B: Receive $1,000 in twelve months with no strings attached.

Choice C: Receive $5,000 in five years.

Choice C seems like a no-brainer, right? You might be right, depending on the overall financial health of Tim and Mary and what their intended use for the funds are. Imagine Tim is a purchasing manager who has a twenty-four hour window to take advantage of a 50% discount on the raw materials his company uses the most of, meaning he could save his company $500, or a net gain of $300 after paying back the additional $200 cost of capital. Mary is the CFO of a startup that just received a significant capital investment and has their expenses covered for the next five years.

The time value of money is the reason Tim would pay to get the money now and while Mary could easily wait five years for the best return. Choice B made little sense for either of them, but with the countless potential business scenarios that arise on a daily basis, it is not hard to see where it could be a viable option for somebody.

## Diminishing Returns

The law of diminishing returns is a concept often misunderstood in economic analysis. Essentially, it indicates that after a certain point, additional inputs yield progressively smaller increments of output. Although this is an illustrative curve and not universally applicable, a common error arises when people rely exclusively on average costs for their analysis. To illustrate the concept, pretend you are working on a project to boost sales and production. The team predicts improvements in profit margins due to the increased production. More products to sell should mean more profits, right? From a macro level overview, the concept seems sound, however, we need to look at all the factors involved in production and not just the output.

To create more finished products, the factory will need more raw materials. There is a cost associated with the additional raw material needed, and the amount could turn out to be more or less than the raw material already on hand. When calculating the raw material costs used in the calculations for determining net profit, we might find the forecasts are created using the average cost of the raw material, which is not the correct approach. Average costs do not accurately reflect the actual expenses in this context.

The cost of raw materials can vary significantly depending on the purchasing volume. In some instances, purchasing more leads to a larger discount, subsequently reducing the cost per unit, which would be favorable for the project. On the other hand, in different circumstances, the cost may escalate with increased purchases, particularly if the raw materials become more expensive as demand grows. Hence, depending on the business model and the pricing dynamics of suppliers, the raw material costs should be calculated based on the expected purchasing volume to obtain a realistic view of the projected profit margins.

Take for instance an individual working with wood products. They draw from an industry where raw material sourcing has direct implications on cost. The primary source of these products is logging. Transportation is a significant expense in this process, with the cost tied closely to the distance the loggers must travel to acquire the timber, the distance to deliver the finished product, and the cost of fuel at any given point in time. As the demand for wood increases, loggers may need to go further to obtain the required timber, incrementally increasing the cost per unit of raw material. This situation emphasizes the importance of calculating costs on incremental or marginal terms rather than relying on an average cost model.

Therefore, it's vital to ensure the costs and revenues used in calculations are based on the incremental or marginal values rather than the average. This approach provides a more accurate reflection of the cost implications of increased purchasing volumes. I cannot simply apply my average sales price to the next 120,000 units, as I may need to offer discounts, or it might not be possible to maintain the same level of savings. One also must consider the additional wear and tear on the machinery needed in production and the associated costs of both maintaining and accounting for any breakdowns. The key takeaway is to avoid relying solely on average pricing.

> **It's vital to ensure the costs and revenues used in calculations are based on the incremental or marginal values rather than the average.**

## Best Practices to Incorporate

Visit www.enablingempowerment.com to download these
tools
  * DMF Excel Financial Model
  * Blogs and articles and applying economic principles
    to decision-making

# 9

# Step 6 - Determine Required Capabilities & Next Steps

**MORE OFTEN THAN** not, the decision-making process is iterative. There won't be just one clear-cut option to choose from, and there likely won't be only one singular way of implementing the option you decide on. That's why we covered the best practices for arriving at the point where we have narrowed down to our best possible options. And at this stage of the process it could become easy to get complacent and just decide on the only remaining option or the one we have a majority vote in favor of. But we still need to think further ahead.

Almost any decision we execute will require some internal capabilities before it can advance to the next step. It might sound like a foregone conclusion, but if the best option requires a substantial capital investment and the organization does not have the available budget/capability, then it has no chance of getting implemented. The larger and more complex the decision at hand is, the more likely you will find yourself faced with capacity restrictions. In these situations, you then need to figure out how to either solve for the lack of capability or pursue a different option that will still bring you closer to implementing the more impactful options as capabilities increase.

If the capabilities are there, we still need to do more strategic planning before it becomes embedded in our business. We need to identify what the next logical steps are for turning the idea into a reality, and often these steps will require pulling in other stakeholders. This is the stage of the DMF where it is not only about deciding if you are able to proceed with the recommendation, but outlining what needs to happen and who will be responsible for what. As the leader and facilitator of the process, it will be your responsibility to decide who the best people are for the job, clearly defining what they will need to do, and then setting realistic timeframes and expectations for completion.

That last part, ensuring satisfactory implementation, will require metrics and KPIs to be thought of and outlined early on in the process. Otherwise, you'll wind up flying by the seat of your pants and it will start to feel like the goal post keeps moving. The KPIs could include milestones by date, budget analysis, manpower hours, or any other objective metrics that are easily tracked and clearly defined. The more closely the KPIs are monitored, the quicker adjustments can be made to get a derailed project back on track or, in a best case scenario, notify relevant stakeholders and end users of a potential faster completion date so all parties are ready when it goes live. Finishing ahead of schedule may seem like it would always be a good problem, but if there is a training or ramp up period needed to use the new process or equipment, those timelines need to be expedited as well.

## Planning Fallacy

**The Planning Fallacy, a term coined by Daniel Kahneman and Amos Tversky, refers to the tendency of individuals or teams to underestimate the time, costs, and risks of future actions while overestimating the benefits.**

In business, particularly in operational roles, effective planning and accurate time estimations are crucial. Yet, many professionals, including myself, have encountered the notorious "Planning Fallacy." This Decision Trap often leads to underestimated timelines and overly optimistic projections, impacting decision-making and eroding organizational trust. The Planning Fallacy, a term coined by Daniel Kahneman and Amos Tversky, refers to the tendency of individuals or teams to underestimate the time, costs, and risks of future actions while overestimating the benefits. This bias affects various domains, from simple daily tasks to complex project management. In a business setting, the Planning Fallacy can lead to missed deadlines, budget overruns, and strained relationships with stakeholders. It's a barrier to realistic planning and can erode confidence in leadership and operational teams.

In Chapter 3, I discussed the challenge I faced due to occasional unplanned equipment downtime during my tenure as the VP of Operations at a large biomass fuel manufacturer, how it contributed to a culture of micromanagement, and how applying the DMF broke the Micromanagement Doom Loop. At the risk of being redundant, I'd like to reexamine that example to illustrate the role the Planning Fallacy played.

As you will recall, frequently, the initial estimates for repair times were overly optimistic. This led to a loss of trust in the operations team when we inevitably missed the forecasted timeline. My initial strategy involved closely monitoring repair progress by requiring the team to provide frequent updates. While this approach yielded some improvement in our ability to hit our estimates, it did not enhance the team's forecasting abilities, and it was personally exhausting. Not to mention that it made my team feel like I didn't trust them, and I'm sure that was very demotivating.

Recognizing that the core issue was overconfidence in best-case scenarios, I implemented a change. Instead of focusing solely on progress monitoring, I asked teams to provide *both best-case and worst-case* repair time estimates, along with factors that could influence these outcomes. This approach led to more accurate forecasts, with repair times generally falling within the estimated range. More importantly, by encouraging the team to focus on what could go wrong in the worst-case scenario, and what they could do to prevent that, repairs frequently were completed much closer to the best-case estimate than the worst-case estimate. By providing a more realistic picture, we regained organizational trust and enhanced our team's forecasting capabilities.

Finally, it broke the micromanagement doom loop and empowered my team to make better decisions about how they could get the equipment back up and running efficiently.

The Planning Fallacy is a pervasive challenge in business operations, but it's not insurmountable. By understanding this bias, applying strategic approaches like range estimates, and utilizing practical tools like the Best/Worst Case Plan, businesses can enhance their forecasting accuracy, rebuild trust, and achieve operational efficiency. To facilitate effective planning and overcome the Planning Fallacy, I developed a "Best/Worst Case Plan" template that can easily be adapted to fit a range of planning scenarios. This template allows teams to:

- Clearly outline best-case and worst-case scenarios
- Identify factors that could lead to each scenario

- Provide a structured approach to forecasting repair times

Here are five other tips for overcoming the Planning Fallacy:

1. Use Ranges for Estimates: Avoid single-point estimates. Provide a range that encompasses best-case and worst-case scenarios.
2. Analyze Past Performances: Reflect on previous similar tasks to guide current estimates.
3. Encourage Team Input: Diverse perspectives can lead to more realistic estimations.
4. Plan for Contingencies: Identify potential pitfalls and include them in planning.
5. Regularly Review and Adjust Estimates: Be flexible and update your timelines based on new information.

## Comparative Advantage

Competitive advantage is an economics principle that your team is not functioning at its most productive capability when individual contributors are working on the thing that they do best, but instead when the people who can do things better than everybody else are allowed to focus on those tasks. It might sound like we are saying the same thing in both instances, so let's use a numerical example to illustrate the difference. In this hypothetical situation, John is a 10/10 when it comes to working on Task A, but he is a 5/10 on Task B. Then we have Sally who is an 8/10 on Task A and a 2/10 on Task B.

The common thought process would be to have John working on Task A, because he is better at it than Sally. But John also happens to be better at Task B, and he does not have the capacity to handle both. This means we have to give Sally either Task A or Task B. To determine who should do what, add up the numerical value of their tasks.

John on Task A: 10
Sally on Task B: 2
Total productivity score: 12

John on Task B: 5
Sally on Task A: 8
Total productivity score: 13

While John may prefer to work on Task A since he has achieved mastery of it, Sally would then be forced to work on Task B where she is barely proficient. Ideally, you will have a well-rounded team of professionals with varying levels of proficiency so you do not find yourself in a situation where you need to assign anyone to a task where they are a 5 or less, figuratively speaking, but in a changing business environment it might happen more than we would like and, until we can help train everyone to the point of proficiency, the best outcome in comparative advantage is achieving the highest team-based score.

To make Step 6 of the DMF as efficient and successful as I have watched it prove to be over the years, there are three best practices to incorporate into process and culture. The first is project segmentation, which involves dividing a large project into manageable tasks. Essentially, it is about identifying the necessary steps required to complete the project. For example, when estimating how long it will take to construct a building, one might reference the timelines of similar past constructions as benchmarks for the current project timeline.

Segmentation entails a detailed inquiry into the various stages of the project timeline, not just a singular focus on the start date and estimated completion date. A good project manager will realize that there are often a sequence of events that must occur in a particular order for the next one to begin. For the process of building a house, or any structure for that matter, project managers should be asking questions such as:

- How long will it take to prepare the ground?
- How much time is needed to lay the foundation?
- How long will constructing the frame take?
- What is the time frame for installing the roof?

By forecasting individually for each of these components and summing them up, you're compelled to consider a wider range of factors than if you were to make a single, overarching estimate. No matter how badly you want to complete the project on schedule, there is no way to skip ahead to working on the roof before the foundation and framing are complete. If I get stuck on a task like writing this book because I am stumped on a particular topic, I have the flexibility to work on a different part of the book to keep pace with my schedule. That is not an option in construction, and any significant delay in the first phase of the project will cause a ripple effect throughout the later stages.

Reference class forecasting is the next best practice to keep in mind. Unlike segmentation, reference class forecasting involves looking at the timelines of analogous projects that have been completed in the past and using that data to predict the duration of the current project. It's a matter of historical comparison—assessing how long similar tasks have taken and applying those lessons to the present work. In considering the procurement and implementation of specialized machinery, such as a widget turner, project timelines are crucial. One might initially estimate that the process will take roughly a year. But it is essential to look into relevant questions for a more accurate projection.

We should inquire:

- How frequently have widget turners been installed in similar settings?
- What has been the historical timeline for such installations?
- What is the computed average duration of these installation projects?

If the anticipated timeline for this new installation significantly deviates from the already known averages, it is incumbent upon the project planners to provide a rationale. They must articulate why this instance is an exception and detail the factors contributing to the differential in the expected time frame.

Finally, we are brought to the best case/worst case theory of planning. The optimal contingency plan incorporates both extreme ends of the spectrum. This approach stems from a template we developed based on past experience. When I began leading operations, we frequently encountered outages. An unexpected equipment failure could halt plant operations completely. In these instances, I was tasked with providing the COO or CEO with timely updates, primarily focusing on when the plant would resume normal function. Upon receiving a notification of an outage, I would immediately contact the plant manager to assess when operations could resume.

If the initial estimate was eight hours of downtime, I would relay this timeline to the leadership. However, should the eight-hour mark pass without resolution—say twelve hours elapsed—I would often find myself fielding follow-up inquiries from the CEO regarding the status of the plant's operations. In seeking updates from the plant manager on the estimated time to restart operations, the reply might reflexively adjust to an additional six-hour wait without any consideration given to why we were already beyond the original estimate. However, on occasion, two days would pass before the plant was fully operational again. During such times, I found myself on the receiving end of significant frustration. The CEO was displeased, expressing concerns over the clear inability to accurately forecast repair timelines.

In response to these events, I established a protocol to mitigate such issues. The updated procedure dictated that if the plant experienced another outage, we would conduct status update calls every two hours. This would allow me to closely monitor progress on repairs and provide more timely and accurate estimates on the resumption of operations. This cycle of events was essentially micromanagement; a natural response given that the plant managers could not accurately predict the repair time frames, which in turn suggested a problem. The inevitable outcome was increased oversight every time an issue arose. Through experience, and with time, the team improved its ability to forecast downtimes and expedited repairs, yet it remained a taxing experience for everyone. Plant managers felt the weight of micromanagement, a perception that was not unfounded.

Personally, the constant updates required, including calls every two hours throughout weekends and nights, were onerous. So, I created a template that comes into play when a machine breaks down. The staff is required to fill it out, which involves breaking down the repair job into individual steps. For each step, they need to provide two estimates: the best-case scenario for the time it will take to complete, and the worst-case scenario. Additionally, they must identify the factors that could cause the timeline to shift from the best to the worst case and come up with mitigation strategies. Moving forward, that became our protocol. Whenever there was an issue and a plant experienced downtime, I would send out the template and request it be completed and returned promptly.

Almost instantly, the accuracy of our time estimates for repairs improved. Actual repair times not only began to consistently fall within the estimated best and worst-case range, but they also tended to be closer to the best-case scenario. This improvement was partly due to asking the team to outline potential worst-case drivers and their respective preventive measures. They proactively devised solutions to mitigate risks before they materialized. Consequently, the CEO was pleased. Instead of having uncertain timelines, such as an initial estimate of twelve hours turning into two days which led to frustration, there was now a more reliable forecast. For example, a communicated estimate might state that the plant would restart operations within 16 to 24 hours, along with a specific list of factors that could extend the timeline to 24 hours instead of 16, and the actions we were taking to prevent those delays.

Consequently, I no longer needed to make two-hour calls when our results were within the projected range; in fact, performance often exceeded expectations. The improvement wasn't due to a change in the team's competence—they were capable all along. The introduction of the template made the difference by eliminating the Planning Fallacy, which previously led to overly optimistic estimates. Utilizing outcome ranges and breaking down tasks allowed the team to provide more accurate forecasts, effectively reducing the need for micromanagement.

## Best Practices to Incorporate

Visit www.enablingempowerment.com to download these tools
- Best-Worst Case Planning Template
- Avoiding the Planning Fallacy Tipsheet

# 10

# Step 7 - Show Your Work

**IN BUSINESS, WE** often focus solely on the outcome of choices—did it succeed or fail? While results are important, true growth relies on analyzing our decision-making processes. That's where Step 7 of Enabling Empowerment's DMF, "Show Your Work," comes into play. By looking beyond just the outcome we can avoid judging a decision by its cover. There is often no correlation between the quality of decision and the effectiveness of its outcome. Much like a gambler in a casino who places a large wager in a game of chance and wins is no more strategic than they are lucky, so too can poor decisions experience luck and yield positive outcomes while strategically sound decisions can backfire due to no fault of the decision-maker.

Documenting your decision-making process is powerful for several reasons. First, it helps combat against the decision trap of Hindsight Bias, which we will explore shortly, by forcing you to revisit your initial assumptions and analysis as circumstances change. Showing your work also improves future decisions by helping you learn from what worked and what needs refining without getting bogged down in only the results. And finally, it provides a clear trail of reasoning, especially in complex situations. If you are ready to get started with implementing a process for showing the work involved in your decision-making process, here are three easy steps to follow:

> **Showing your work also improves future decisions by helping you learn from what worked and what needs refining without getting bogged down in only the results.**

1. Capture: Write down the key factors, data, and assumptions you considered.

2. Analyze: Document your thought process. How did you weigh different options?
3. Reflect: After the results are in, honestly analyze your original decision-making process.

The Bottom Line is that documenting your work isn't about placing blame or proving you were always right. It's about becoming a more strategic, self-aware decision-maker. When you embrace the process, not just the results, becoming more thorough is like second nature. If a decision does not turn out the way you expected, you can reference back to the criteria used in the process and determine where things went wrong. You may even find that you did everything right and the failure was a result of factors outside your control, a reassuring confidence boost you would otherwise not have without following the documentation process.

> **It's about becoming a more strategic, self-aware decision-maker.**

This leads us to the importance of validating the actual results we have produced and not simply assuming they are good or bad because they met or missed our expectations. Having some criteria to validate the quality of our results serves two primary purposes. First, it is about documenting the process in a manner that facilitates easy presentation to others, garnering their buy-in. This could be an approver, a necessary supporter, or perhaps someone whose input or challenge you seek to test your strategy against. Proper documentation supports these interactions.

Second, with particular regard to the Decision Trap of Hindsight Bias, it is crucial to record our initial assumptions, perceived risks, and needs. This way, when we later review our decisions to evaluate their efficacy, we will not fall prey to assuming we could have known things that were not knowable at the time. It's about preserving the context of our decisions for accurate retrospective analysis. By recording those assumptions, we create reference points we can revisit in the future for assessment. This supports the principle that the quality of a decision should be judged based on the information available and the analysis conducted at the time it was made. This process provides us with the chance to capture what we knew at that specific moment.

**The quality of a decision should be judged based on the information available and the analysis conducted at the time it was made.**

## Hindsight Bias

There is a common tendency for people to perceive past events as having been more predictable than they actually were. People often believe that after an event has occurred, they would have predicted or perhaps even would have known with a high degree of certainty what the outcome of the event would have been before the event occurred. Hindsight bias may cause distortions of memories of what was known or believed before an event occurred, and is a significant source of overconfidence (remember that trap?) regarding an individual's ability to predict the outcomes of future events.

Hindsight Bias is more likely to occur when the outcome of an event is negative rather than positive. This is a phenomenon consistent with the general tendency for people to pay more attention to negative outcomes of events than positive outcomes. In addition, Hindsight Bias is affected by the severity of the negative outcome. In malpractice lawsuits, it has been found that the more severe a negative outcome is, the juror's Hindsight Bias is more dramatic. In a perfectly objective case, the verdict would be based on the physician's standard of care instead of the outcome of the treatment; however, studies show that cases ending in severe negative outcomes (such as death) result in a higher level of Hindsight Bias.

Let's think about a company that must choose which of two similar products to produce and sell. Its marketers are absolutely certain Product A has a 70% chance of yielding a $1 million profit, while Product B has a 80% chance of yielding a $1 million profit. Company executives choose Product B, but it ends up not only missing the mark on the million dollar profit target, but actually leads to a slight loss. Later that year, the company's main competitor markets Product A and makes about $1 million in profit. On scale of 1-8, was the company's decision to produce and market Product B clearly the wrong decision (1) or clearly the right decision (8)?

As another example, in 1996, Susan and Gary LaBine[10] proposed a scenario where a psychiatric patient told a therapist that he was contemplating harming another individual. The therapist did not warn the other individual of the possible danger. Participants were each given one of three possible outcomes: the threatened individual either received no injuries, minor injuries, or serious injuries. Participants were then asked to determine if the physician should be considered negligent. Participants in the "serious injuries" condition were not only more likely to rate the therapist as negligent but also rated the attack as more foreseeable. Participants in the no injuries and minor injury categories were more likely to see the therapist's actions as reasonable.

## Recallability Trap

The Recallability Trap is very similar to the Availability Trap, except it focuses on what one can remember and not the information at their disposal. Because we frequently base our predictions about future events on our memory of past events, we can be overly influenced by dramatic events—those that leave a strong impression on our memory. This same trigger also causes us to exaggerate the probability of rare but catastrophic occurrences such as plane crashes because they get disproportionate attention in the media.

In one experiment, lists of well-known men and women were read to different groups of people. Unbeknownst to the subjects, each list had an equal number of men and women, but on some lists the men were more famous than the women while on others the women were more famous. Afterward, the participants were asked to estimate the percentages of men and women on each list. Those who had heard the list with the more famous men thought there were more men on the list, while those who had heard the one with the more famous women thought there were more women.

Corporate lawyers often get caught in the Recallability Trap when defending liability suits. Their decisions about whether to settle a claim or take it to court usually hinge on their assessments of the possible outcomes of a trial. Because the media tend to aggressively publicize massive damage awards (while ignoring other, far more common trial outcomes), lawyers can overestimate the probability of a large award for the plaintiff. As a result, they offer larger settlements than are actually warranted.

To minimize the distortion caused by variations in recallability, carefully examine all your assumptions to ensure they're not unduly influenced by your memory. Get actual statistics whenever possible. Try not to be guided by impressions. In short, do your due diligence and put in the work. Even those who have the best memories in the world stand to make errors in judgment when they accept their recollection of events as fact. Even if they are clear and accurate, there is still no guarantee the same results can be expected in the current situation you are solving for.

## Best Practices to Incorporate

Visit www.enablingempowerment.com to download these tools
- DMF Summary Template
- DMF Discussion Reminder Card

10. Labine, Susan J., and Gary Labine. "Determinations of Negligence and the Hindsight Bias." Law and Human Behavior 20, no. October 1996 (1996): 501-516. Accessed March 31, 2024. https://www.ojp.gov/ncjrs/virtual-library/abstracts/determinations-negligence-and-hindsight-bias.

# 11

# Creating a Culture of Principled Entrepreneurship

**CULTURE CHANGE IS** one topic that has no shortage of coverage. It feels like a billion books have been written on the subject, and everybody seems to have varied opinions about what it is, what the ideal state is, and how to achieve it. One of the most significant problems with culture though, is that it tends to be thought of as a buzzword—if you use the word "culture" enough it will magically become a real thing at all levels of the organization. Clearly, that is not the case, and we are starting to find that more leaders than ever before are beginning to recognize how important it is to deliberately manage the culture within their organizations.

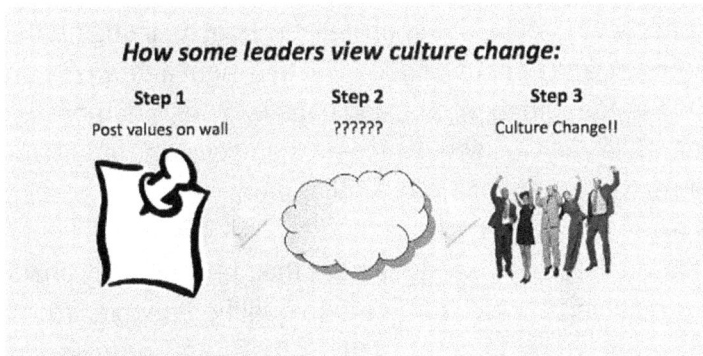

*How some leaders view culture change:*

| Step 1 | Step 2 | Step 3 |
|---|---|---|
| Post values on wall | ?????? | Culture Change!! |

A notable survey[11] originally conducted by Booz and Company in 2013, and later republished by PWC, found that *84% of respondents agreed that their organization's culture is critical to business success.* The same survey found that *96% of respondents said that some change to their culture is needed, and 51% believe it needs a major overhaul.* Unfortunately, many leaders feel ill-equipped to initiate the necessary culture change. I rarely have clients argue that the culture of their organization does not need to change. More commonly, their question is: "How should we go about it?"

In answering this question, I have found that it can be very useful to look to the church as a role model for structuring their company's cultural transformation. The reality is, if you just take an objective look, there are no organizations that are better at crafting a common culture than religious institutions. If you really want to understand how to create a group of people with shared beliefs and behaviors, then you might as well take a leaf out of the religious institutions' book. The strategies of these religious organizations that synagogues, churches, mosques, or other houses of worship employ with their congregations are time-tested in building powerful, collective cultures. By definition, a religion is a group of people who share common beliefs about their origins, their purposes, and notions of good and bad, right and wrong, and how they should think, act, and behave. What's humorous is that, while each religion considers themselves different from the rest, each one has very similar practices.

What do they do? They document their beliefs. They ensure that teachings come from certain qualified people. To join, you must stand in front of the others and profess your adherence to these beliefs. And if you can't subscribe to these tenets, then, well, they suggest you leave. No one thinks this is crazy when they attend a religious ceremony or rite of passage, and the business world would be better off for embodying some of these principles into the underlying corporate culture. There are six specific lessons I like to focus on when making this comparison between secular and non-secular organizations, especially in the context of what we can do.

1.  They write down what they believe: All religions have written text that documents what they believe.

Moreover, these texts are sacred; only a select few have the authority to change them. The documents are treated with respect. They are read and studied diligently. They are even memorized and recited. If you desire to create a strong organizational culture in your company, start by writing down what you believe. Put governance in place to control who can make changes to the document. Encourage people to study, learn, and even memorize the document.

2. They have levels of authority for interpreting and teaching what they believe: Most churches require that teachers, pastors, ministers, and other church leadership be educated on the sacred text and understand its meaning. The church understands the importance of having leaders interpret the text consistently, thus they educate and test them on their basic understanding before giving them authority to teach the congregation. Similarly, they understand the importance of leaders modeling behaviors that are consistent with their beliefs. Their training and process of appointing leaders is designed to eliminate people who don't behave in a manner consistent with their beliefs. Similarly, companies that create a strong culture, invest time in training their leaders to speak and behave consistently with the beliefs and values they want all employees to share.

3. They don't let just anyone join their church: In order to become a member of most churches, you are required to attend a class, or series of classes, teaching the specific beliefs of that particular congregation. In addition, one is typically required to make a public statement of sorts professing their beliefs are consistent with the beliefs of the church.

Companies that create a strong culture utilize processes like behavior-based interviews to screen employees to determine if they behave consistently with their particular values. Likewise, they send new hires through an orientation process ensuring they understand the company values and expectations.

4. They utilize symbols and rituals to remind people of their beliefs: Churches utilize statues, stained glass windows, banners, and other symbols to remind members of specific beliefs and to evoke emotions. Similarly they use rituals such as prayers, holidays, special meals, and songs to unite members and keep their beliefs at the forefront of their minds. Companies that want to create a strong culture can utilize similar techniques by creating images, graphics, and other artifacts that remind employees of particular corporate values. They utilize rituals by having routine company meetings, periodic celebrations, or annual awards ceremonies.

5. There are rewards for behaving consistently with the beliefs: Behaving consistently with the church's beliefs results in increased esteem and recognition from its leaders and members. It may even mean being asked to hold special positions of leadership or authority. Likewise, in companies with a strong organizational culture, the leaders recognize, reward, and promote those employees that behave consistently with the desired values and beliefs.

6. There are punishments for behaving inconsistently with beliefs, up to and including dismissal. If you don't behave consistently with the beliefs of the church, you will be confronted by its leaders and fellow members. They don't just look the other way. Typically,

they will initially reach out to help and support the misguided member. However, a sustained pattern of misbehavior will eventually result in banishment from the congregation. Similarly, leaders that create a strong organizational culture do not ignore behavior that is inconsistent with their company's values. They confront it with empathy and compassion. However, if an employee's behavior doesn't change accordingly, they are subject to dismissal.

If those are not compelling enough reasons for looking to the church as a benchmark for creating a lasting organizational culture, let's look at some of the ways these institutions can provide guidance on the five steps needed for creating a culture of Principled Entrepreneurship that thrives on trust and calculated risk-taking while avoiding micromanagement, which stifles innovation, creates bottlenecks, and leads to disengaged employees. Empowering individuals to make data-driven decisions unlocks their potential, fostering a collaborative culture of creativity and progress. Building this culture of Principled Entrepreneurship may take time and effort, but the long-term benefits significantly outweigh any challenges. When employees act like owners, innovation flourishes, customer focus deepens, and value creation becomes embedded in your company's DNA.

> **When employees act like owners, innovation flourishes, customer focus deepens, and value creation becomes embedded in your company's DNA.**

At Enabling Empowerment, we strive to show organizations the simple five-step roadmap as to how they can create a culture of principled entrepreneurship. The next five sections of this chapter will cover those steps and, with the exception of the Defining the Culture and Measuring the Culture, both of which can be done interchangeably, they should be implemented chronologically.

## Define the Culture

Let's begin by defining organizational culture. Perhaps the most widely accepted definition of "organizational culture" comes from Edgar Schein. He defines culture as "a pattern of shared basic assumptions that the group learned as it solved its problems of external adaptation and internal integration, that has worked well enough to be considered valid and, therefore, to be taught to new members as the correct way to perceive, think, and feel in relation to those problems."

From this definition, we see that, at its core, an organizational culture is a set of "shared basic assumptions." What better example of an organization with a strongly shared set of basic assumptions can you think of than your local religious institution? This is not meant to be irreverent or condescending in any way. I am not endorsing or denigrating any particular church or religion. I'm simply pointing out that if you want to examine an organization that has a very closely-held and strongly-shared set of beliefs, then look no further than your local house of worship, regardless of the particular faith, doctrine, or denomination. Members of each congregation are empowered to share their faith with all they come in contact with and feel morally responsible for living up to the standards set by those who have created the framework for their beliefs.

Now that we know what the definition of culture is, we need to think about how we can define the culture of our own organization. Defining your culture isn't just about slapping a mission statement on the wall. It's about digging deep and articulating the values that should guide every decision, every interaction, every aspect of how your company operates. Think of it as your organization's moral compass, helping you navigate tricky situations and stay true to your purpose. When we talk about a culture of Principled Entrepreneurship, we're talking about a set of values that empower employees to act like owners. But what does that look like in practice? Here are a few examples of value statements that might define such a culture:

> **Defining your culture isn't just about slapping a mission statement on the wall. It's about digging deep and articulating the values that should guide every decision, every interaction, every aspect of how your company operates.**

- **Ownership Mentality:** Principled entrepreneurs view themselves as owners of their work, not just employees. They demonstrate personal responsibility for outcomes, take pride in their contributions, and proactively invest in the company's long-term success.
- **Continuous Learning:** Principled entrepreneurs are driven by a relentless curiosity, always excited to acquire new knowledge, skills, and perspectives. They understand that learning is the key to adaptability, improvement, and finding innovative solutions to challenges.
- **Bias for Action:** Principled entrepreneurs don't let analysis paralysis hold them back. They courageously embrace calculated risk-taking,

prioritize experimentation, and learn from successes and failures as stepping stones toward progress.

- **Customer Obsession:** Principled entrepreneurs recognize that delivering exceptional value to customers is the heart of sustainable business. They go beyond meeting basic needs, deeply understanding their customers' pain points, and exceeding expectations.
- **Integrity and Trust:** Principled entrepreneurs act with unwavering ethics, honesty, and transparency. They understand that trust is the foundation of strong relationships with customers, colleagues, and stakeholders, and they consistently behave in ways that build and maintain this trust.

The specific values you choose will depend on your unique company and its aspirations, so please just use the ones above as a guide or starting point.

---

To truly define your culture, you can't just have leaders dictate from on high. You need to involve your team in the process and build a shared definition. Here's a simple but effective exercise I've used with many clients:

1. Gather Key Stakeholders: Bring together a diverse group of employees from different levels and departments.
2. Brainstorm Values: Ask each person to write down the values and behaviors they want to see in the future culture on sticky notes.

3. Group and Refine: Have everyone stick their notes on a whiteboard and group similar statements together.
4. Craft Guiding Principles: As a group, distill each cluster of sticky notes into a concise value statement that captures the essence of what you want your culture to be.

In today's dynamic business landscape, empowering employees to act as Principled Entrepreneurs can yield extraordinary returns, and this collaborative approach not only helps you define it, but also builds excitement, ownership, and a shared sense of purpose among the team. When people feel like they have had a hand in shaping the culture, they are far more likely to embrace it and make it a reality. This philosophy transcends traditional top-down management and cultivates a sense of ownership, innovation, and long-term value creation within a company.

Before we can explore what this culture involves, its profound benefits, and how to implement it within your organization, we must first define exactly what a culture of principled entrepreneurship is, which is a term first coined by Koch Industries. This type of culture fosters an environment where employees are empowered to think and act like owners of the business, taking initiative, embracing calculated risks, and making decisions aligned with the company's mission and values.

**This type of culture fosters an environment where employees are empowered to think and act like owners of the business, taking initiative, embracing calculated risks, and making decisions aligned with the company's mission and values.**

If creating something that sounds so complex feels like more trouble than it might be worth, we need to take a step back and look at the benefits that come from putting in the work. The first benefit comes by way of enhanced agility and innovation on the part of our employees. Principled Entrepreneurs are closer to customer needs, market trends, and the source of problems. This enables them to make rapid, informed decisions, leading to greater adaptability in an ever-changing world. It also increases employee engagement by creating a culture of autonomy and ownership that cultivates passion, dedication, and a sense of purpose, resulting in higher levels of employee satisfaction and retention. And most importantly, it creates superior long-term value by shifting the focus from short-term wins to sustainable business models that deliver enduring success.

## Measure the Culture

The first step on this journey toward creating a culture of Principled Entrepreneurship is a crucial one. Before you can adequately measure anything, we must first have a firm understanding of where we are starting from, and that begins by assessing the current culture of your organization. Only by gaining a clear picture of your organization's existing values, norms, and behaviors can you craft a truly effective transformation plan. One of the best ways I have found to achieve this over the course of my career has been to create a culture assessment.

Performing this culture assessment is important for many reasons, but three main ones stand out above all others. The first is for providing a baseline of understanding for the starting point in your journey by highlighting both the strengths you can build upon and the areas in need of improvement. Second, the assessment eliminates a propensity toward bias through a data-driven approach. To accomplish this, informed decision-making is essential. Assessments provide qualitative and quantitative data, giving you a better understanding of your culture's intricacies and removing the emotion. And last but not least is something we touched upon in the prior section—increasing employee

> **A well-designed assessment demonstrates to employees that their voices matter, fostering buy-in from the outset of the change process.**

engagement. A well-designed assessment demonstrates to employees that their voices matter, fostering buy-in from the outset of the change process.

There are two main ways an organization can go about performing these types of cultural assessments. Traditional culture assessments often rely on surveys as one of the main sources of insight into current conditions. While surveys can be helpful, they can also feel impersonal and may not fully capture the nuances of your team's experiences. This is where the strategy of having "focused culture discussions" offers a powerful alternative.

This strategy is most effective when following these four simple steps:

Leadership-led Discussions: Assign leaders to conduct one-on-one conversations with team members using a structured discussion guide (an example of this tool is available at www.enablingempowerment.com).

Targeted Questions: The guide combines standard questions to gauge perceptions of core cultural beliefs with open-ended questions focused on strengths, weaknesses, barriers, and solutions.

Data Analysis and Action Planning: After the discussions, leadership analyzes the collective feedback to identify themes, generate solutions to overcome barriers, and enhance positive cultural attributes.

Feedback Loop: The results and action plan are transparently shared with the team, inviting their input and further solidifying their participation in the culture change process.

While surveys will always be part of the management-employee feedback loop and provide areas of insights, I advocate having focused culture discussions for the inherent benefits it provides above and beyond what an anonymous survey might be able to capture. The most obvious benefit is the focus on dialogue over data. This method prioritizes honest conversations, fostering a connection between leaders and employees that surveys cannot match. It also demonstrates commitment on the part of leadership by openly asking team members for their candid feedback. This signals leadership's genuine commitment to creating a better workplace instead of keeping survey results to themselves with no promise of ever acting on them. And one of the most important benefits in my opinion is that it fosters collaboration. Sharing the analysis and collaboratively building action plans reinforces the idea that everyone plays a role in shaping the desired culture.

## Culture Transformation Plan

If we determine that part of the culture we want to have within our organization is for people to be able to make better decisions, we need to have an understanding of how comfortable they currently are with making decisions of varying importance. We may or may not have gotten a sense of those answers during the defining and measuring processes, but if that has not happened, this would be the time to start asking the employees direct questions. Ideally, the feedback will tell us that they are already "very confident" in decision-making, but we all know nothing is ideal.

Once we have their feedback, we need to put together an action plan for boosting confidence. Important to note that this action plan will likely not be a one-size-fits-all approach. Based on where each of your employees fell on the confidence spectrum, the plan should be tailored to some degree. That's not to say all 400 people in an organization need to have personalized plans, just that there should be some differentiation between the plan for someone who has virtually zero confidence and someone who has higher than average confidence with room to gain more. Otherwise, those on the lower end of the spectrum will feel overwhelmed and those toward the higher end might not feel challenged enough.

We need to close the confidence gap through training programs and changes to the processes that reinforce a culture of confident decision-making. When I work with organizations to purposefully drive a culture change, we use the information from our assessment to come up with specific actions to address that feedback, not theory. Then, three months later, we go back and assess again to see how we are doing and if the culture change happened. By repeating that cycle over and over again, you continue to show people this culture is important and you are committed to building the strongest one possible.

## Communicate the Culture

Based on all the positive impacts my DMF has had on organizations, many have also reached out to me for assistance in altering their corporate cultures. For effective client service, it became clear that I needed to devise a replicable process to better serve my growing clientèle. This led me to explore methods for documenting and defining an organization's culture. One key aspect was determining how to communicate cultural change and articulate an organization's ethos through various mediums, such as role description sheets. Many organizations emphasize the value of a questioning attitude, but the challenge lies in conveying this to operators in practical terms. It's one thing to tell an operator to have a questioning attitude; it's entirely another to specify the behaviors that embody this mindset in their daily responsibilities.

The goal is to make the abstract tangible: to clarify exactly which behaviors are expected to change. This forms a connection with the workers, because merely espousing the value of a questioning attitude without concrete actions is unlikely to result in any real transformation. As much as understanding the organizational value of empowerment is pivotal in shaping corporate culture, it has to be done with precision. If employees, such as operators or frontline staff handling phone calls, are simply told that empowerment is important, they're often left uncertain about what that means in the real sense.

To make it concrete, let's refine the expectation. Rather than having staff members routinely ask direct supervisors for directives, have the most senior levels of management openly encourage them to proactively present their recommendations. When it is delivered in such a way, everyone is on the same page. Workers at the most basic level understand that those at the highest level expect everyone to contribute to problem solving initiatives and there will be less fear of backlash from their department heads when they show initiative. This specific behavior reflects the core value of the organization endorsing its members to autonomously make decisions. This is the pragmatic approach that I developed and fine-tuned the tools for cultural transformation that I now employ.

I think most people believe they are doing a decent job of communicating expectations around culture throughout their organization. But if you believe that and the current process looks something like having a town hall meeting where the leader stands up with a couple PowerPoint slides and explains what their values are, and maybe what they mean—you are missing the mark. If you are tacking posters and other artifacts that communicate and remind people of the desired values as a follow up to those

**While these behaviors are better than doing nothing, they aren't good enough.**

town hall meetings, you are getting slightly better. While these behaviors are better than doing nothing, they aren't good enough. At the end of the day, they don't make it to the people on the front lines or transfer into very specific behaviors expected of them in how they work. They just become additional items for people to check off a list and say they have attended or reviewed the material.

One of the most effective ways I have found to communicate the culture is by using role description sheets (an example of this tool is available at www.enablingempowerment.com). These are documents that translate the cultural value statements into specific behaviors that are or are not aligned with the value statements when performing specific tasks. Someone in a leadership role will sit down with each person in their role and go through the values. If we decide ownership is one of our values, we record it as a defined value for our desired culture. Then, we review each role. For instance, we might describe behaviors that are and are not aligned to the value statement "Seek to Understand Others' Points of View" when a Customer Service Representative is dealing with a customer complaint. The best way to develop these is in a workshop format with groups of employees in the same role building out the role description sheets for tasks they frequently perform. This not only helps to align them all on the behaviors that are expected, it creates a reference document that can be referred back to when giving them performance feedback.

We need to get very detailed and practical with what the value looks like in the day-to-day work of each department or division and give real world examples they can understand. So yes, have a town hall and hang the posters, but also make sure leaders are having these one-on-one conversations with employees and giving them specific examples of behaviors aligned with the desired culture and behaviors that are not aligned to it. Don't rush through the process to check another box off the list. Actively listen to each of the employees and take what they say under advisement. If enough people believe something to be a value that you had not previously considered, it might be time to reevaluate for that department or possibly the entire company.

When leaders are trying to change a culture, they need to advertise the behaviors aligned with the new culture as well. If we want to foster a culture where employees are expected to question things that don't seem right, one of the ways to support this is by not reacting poorly when someone shares bad news from something they questioned. As a leader, I would make an effort to not react poorly when someone brings me bad news when I should be celebrating them for having the difficult conversation I asked them to have. If I do react poorly, I want someone to point out to me that I'm not embodying the behaviors aligned with the values. Going forward, when I act in accordance with the value, I will point out to the other person that I didn't react poorly because I want people to feel they can question things. When you are in a business where the previous culture was defined by leaders reacting poorly to bad news, reacting properly one time doesn't erase the thousand wrong moves from the past, because change takes place over time, and people need to get acclimated and comfortable to the new culture you are building.

## Integrate Into Management System

While the culture transformation plan and our efforts to communicate the desired culture are critical to driving the initial shift values and behaviors, long-term sustainability of culture change requires embedding the new behaviors into your management processes.

The processes you use to manage your business, ultimately shape your culture. The behaviors that your management processes encourage will be reinforced, and the behaviors that are punished will be discouraged. Therefore, we need to make sure that our management processes encourage the new values and behaviors we have defined.

For instance, if our management processes have many layers of approval built into them, this can discourage employees from taking initiative or feeling "ownership" for their decisions. Similarly, if our annual performance review process, and our compensation strategy, doesn't reward people for taking on risk, then it will continue to discourage those behaviors.

Discussing all the ways your management processes can be altered to reinforce your desired culture of Principled Entrepreneurship, let's focus on what I believe to be one of the most powerful concepts, which is Decision Rights.

## Decision Rights

Decision Rights are the authority and responsibility assigned to individuals to make specific decisions, and they should be granted based on an individual's knowledge, expertise, and demonstrated competence, as well as the potential impact of the decision on a company's overall performance, allowing us to make calculated choices. Say, in teaching someone to swim, there is a difference between the manageable environment of a shallow pool and the unpredictable nature of the open ocean. In the former, the water is just deep enough to swim but still safe enough for a quick rescue. In contrast, the ocean presents real dangers that may not afford a second chance. This is analogous to how we handle the delegation of decision-making power in transforming an organization's culture. It is about striking a balance between giving enough room to learn from real decisions and ensuring that these decisions won't have catastrophic consequences.

> **Decision Rights are the authority and responsibility assigned to individuals to make specific decisions, and they should be granted based on an individual's knowledge, expertise, and demonstrated competence, as well as the potential impact of the decision on a company's overall performance, allowing us to make calculated choices.**

First, I provide the opportunity to make choices that, even if they go wrong, can be corrected and learned from, without causing lasting damage. Gradually, as competence and confidence build, the scope and scale of the decisions can grow. We can recover if there are any missteps. As you demonstrate competence, such as passing the swimming test in the five-foot end of the pool, we'll move on to bigger challenges, like the diving tank. Once you've mastered that, we'll progress to swimming in a lake, and then ultimately the open ocean. The point is, we'll gradually scale up the complexity and the stakes of the tasks.

Decision Rights, a term coined by Charles Koch, refers to the specific levels of authority individuals hold within an organization. For example, in many companies, plant managers are often given identical spending authority regardless of their plant's size or needs. They might each have the approval to authorize expenditures up to $50,000. This spending limit is usually standardized across all plant managers and doesn't typically change. Koch Industries has adopted a unique approach that encourages individual initiative and entrepreneurial thinking. This is achieved through a system where Decision Rights are directly linked to an individual's displayed aptitude for making prudent decisions, rather than just their role or title.

For example, let's consider a typical career trajectory at Georgia Pacific, a subsidiary of Koch Industries. When an employee is promoted to a plant manager, they might initially be granted the authority to approve requisitions and expenses up to $10,000. This financial limit essentially sets the boundary for their autonomous decision-making. Should any costs exceed the $10,000 threshold, the plant manager must seek the green light from someone higher up in the chain of command, such as the regional operations director. The director, due to their broader oversight and proven decision-making skills, would have a greater spending authority, perhaps up to $75,000.

But the escalation doesn't stop there. Above the regional operations director, there may be another tier of management with an even wider scope for decision-making. This next level—perhaps a vice president—would have authority over considerably larger sums, up to $250,000. And further up the hierarchy, a senior executive might wield the power to approve transactions and investments as high as $1 million. By structuring Decision Rights in this manner, Koch Industries incentivizes its employees to refine their decision-making abilities. As they demonstrate competency and the aptitude to handle greater responsibilities, they are entrusted with more significant spending authority, paving the way for a meritocratic advancement system. This not only empowers individuals to work with an entrepreneurial mindset but also aligns with the company's vision of rewarding talent and skill.

As a new plant manager, I often found myself passing requisition requests exceeding my $10,000 limit to the regional operations director for approval. Each time, I would have to justify the expenditure by calling him and explaining my reasoning in detail. During these discussions, I would outline the problem I was aiming to solve, enumerate the different options I had weighed, and identify the primary factors influencing my decision. I talked through how I planned to mitigate risks, the expected returns on the investment, and so forth.

After going through this process about half a dozen times, the regional operations director recognized the consistency and rigor in my decision-making. He was impressed and told me, "Chris, you've demonstrated a solid decision-making process each time you've called. You don't need to run these by me anymore. I'm confident in your judgment, and I'm transferring my $75,000 decision rights to you."

This was a pivotal moment that exemplified the trust and empowerment Koch Industries promotes, proving that as employees showcase their decision-making capabilities, they can earn more autonomy and responsibility. By looking at the bigger picture and not simply adhering to a rigid structure someone wrote into their operations manual as a catchall, Koch Industries allowed their people with the right levels of skills and expertise to have greater autonomy instead of only focusing on those who might have been at a higher level in terms of job title or pay grade.

In a similar fashion, as I continued to exhibit sound judgment and decision-making prowess, I was able to take on even more responsibility. There came a point when I no longer needed to consult with the regional operations director for expenditures exceeding $75,000. After a series of successful larger-scale requisitions, he conveyed his confidence in me by elevating my decision rights to $150,000. Because my DMF was, as he called it, "robust and reliable," I no longer had to seek out his approval.

While I was progressing, there were other plant managers who weren't as adept at articulating the rationale behind their spending decisions, especially when it came to significant dollar amounts. Because they didn't demonstrate the same level of competence in their decision-making, their authority to make financial decisions remained unchanged. The overarching principle of this approach is in incentivizing you to hone your decision-making skills and effectively communicate the logic behind them. By successfully doing this, you're rewarded with increased authority and autonomy, eliminating the need to constantly seek approvals for your initiatives. This system encourages personal growth and efficiency, as your increased Decision Rights are reflective of your proven expertise.

> **The overarching principle of this approach is in incentivizing you to hone your decision-making skills and effectively communicate the logic behind them.**

Conversely, if a company were to maintain static decision rights across the board, it could potentially stifle innovation and motivation. When everyone has the same level of decision-making power, regardless of their expertise or ability to justify their choices, there's less drive for individuals to improve or excel. It's crucial for an organization's success to recognize and empower those who develop and demonstrate superior decision-making capabilities. When people can easily see the benefits of being more autonomous and how the added responsibility can actually make their lives easier, it is a win for them and a win for the organization. If it is a customer-facing role, it becomes a win for the customer as well.

**When everyone has the same level of decision-making power, regardless of their expertise or ability to justify their choices, there's less drive for individuals to improve or excel.**

In the context of most companies, spending authority is often just a fixed approval limit set uniformly for everyone. When this limit is standardized, it tends to have a dual downside. On one hand, individuals who lack strong decision-making skills may be granted more authority than they can handle responsibly. On the other hand, those who are adept at making decisions are not given sufficient authority to fully utilize their potential and feel motivated. By treating Decision Rights not as a given, but rather as a privilege that's earned, it changes the entire dynamic. This concept implies that the capacity to make larger and more impactful decisions is something to be attained through demonstrating competence and trustworthiness. It's a merit-based system that rewards analytical skills and good judgment, thereby fostering a more proactive and skilled management team.

Taking money out of the equation, there are also plenty of other situations where discretionary decision-making rights can benefit the organization. In many of the plants I visit, there is a standard procedure mandating a frontline supervisor to notify the operations manager if a piece of equipment has been inoperable for two hours. This rule is applied universally, regardless of the supervisor's experience or capability. However, this one-size-fits-all rule doesn't account for the varying skill levels of the supervisors. Some supervisors, especially those who are new, inexperienced, or less proficient, might benefit from calling the operations manager much sooner, perhaps within 15 minutes of the downtime. This early intervention can help mitigate issues before they escalate.

Conversely, there are seasoned supervisors with a wealth of experience and the proficiency to tackle these situations effectively. When they make the two-hour call, they often have already devised a strategy and have the situation well in hand. In such cases, it may be wise for the operations manager to trust their judgment and give them the autonomy to manage the issue without unnecessary oversight. They will be the first ones to know if the scope of the problem is beyond their ability and in need of outside support, or if their team already has the necessary tools and resources, even if the expected outage might take three hours to repair. Just think about the time wasted in making the call, explaining an issue you know how to fix, and then waiting for a technician who is going to do exactly what you would have started an hour ago.

It's important to customize the directive based on each supervisor's demonstrated capabilities. For a highly proficient supervisor, the threshold for escalating a shutdown to the operations manager might be extended to four hours, giving them leeway to resolve the issue without intervention. In contrast, a less experienced or less effective supervisor should reach out much sooner, say after twenty minutes of downtime, as they haven't yet shown the ability to manage such situations independently. When you demonstrate increasing competence, you will likely be granted greater levels of jurisdiction. I want to give my people enough leeway to learn from their mistakes, while ensuring those mistakes are not so consequential that we can't recover from them.

This approach is not merely for the benefit of those looking to improve their decision-making skills but also serves as a broader message to organizations currently imposing rigid controls on their decision-making processes. This message is for the executives and leaders who may wonder how to best implement this strategy without assuming undue risk. The idea is not to abruptly relinquish control and expect immediate mastery of decision-making from the team. Rather, it is about establishing a thoughtful progression, delegating incrementally more authority as individuals prove their capability.

This strategy recognizes that skill acquisition is not uniform— some might progress quickly, able to manage high-stakes decisions soon, akin to scuba diving in open waters. Others may take longer, possibly staying in the metaphorical kiddie pool for a year, cautiously building up their expertise. But either way, this method fosters motivation. If team members understand they can gain more autonomy by effectively justifying their decisions, they have a tangible incentive to improve swiftly. After all, no one relishes the need to constantly seek their superior's approval before acting. Encouraging team members to be proactive and self-reliant is beneficial for all parties involved.

11. "Culture's Role in Enabling Organizational Change: Survey Ties Transformation Success to Deft Handling of Cultural Issues." Booz & Company, (2013). Accessed March 31, 2024. https://www.strategyand.pwc.com/gx/en/insights/2002-2013/cultures-role/strategyand-cultures-role-in-enabling-organizational-change.pdf.

# Conclusion

**IN CASE YOU** haven't figured it out already, there is no quick fix to improving your business. Whether it be increasing sales, decreasing expenses, driving safety initiatives, or improving the overall company culture, you need to put in the work to empower your people to make better autonomous decisions. You are not going to make more money by simply selling more products or reducing costs. You are not going to increase safety initiatives by holding more perfunctory meetings or assigning training courses without any real world application. Focusing on these temporary fixes will only land you in more trouble down the road.

To bring about significant positive change you need to make more investment decisions that result in positive returns than you do ones that result in negative returns. And this cannot only be expected from those at the top. Sure, most of the larger financial decisions are handled at upper management, but just think about how many decisions your frontline employees make every day and the potential cost or benefit the company can realize when they are also making better decisions that result in positive returns.

If you aren't going to make more quality decisions at every level of the organization, then you're not going to have a successful business. It is incredible how so many organizations in this day and age still do not have a formal strategy to make good decisions or focus on making it a core competency for their organization. I think it's widely understood that empowering your people to make decisions will lead to better decision-making, but even fewer companies have any type of strategy on how to do that either. They think they can do it just by waving their hands and watching it magically come into existence. Unfortunately, that doesn't work. We need a formal strategy to make it a core competency, and that's what I have laid out in this book. By teaching people a common Decision-Making Framework, we teach them how to avoid Decision Traps and become more autonomous.

You can't begin to create a culture where people are empowered to make decisions until you've given them the necessary skills and capabilities to do so. If you walk into an organization and say you're empowering everyone to make decisions but you haven't taught them the framework, you're setting yourself up for failure. You're going to make it worse than it was before, and you're going to get a bunch of terrible recommendations and decisions. The good news is that this should no longer feel like rocket science or nuclear propulsion after reading this book and following the 7 *Steps of the DMF*.

# About the Author

Chris Seifert is a seasoned operations executive and leadership consultant with a proven track record of driving operational excellence and cultural transformation in diverse industries. His career spans over three decades, encompassing leadership roles in the U.S. Navy's Nuclear Submarine Force, plant management positions at Georgia-Pacific and Owens Corning, and executive leadership at a leading biomass energy company. As a Partner at Wilson Perumal & Company, Chris founded and grew their Operational Excellence practice, serving dozens of multi-billion-dollar companies in the Oil and Gas, Chemical, and other high-hazard industries.

Chris's expertise lies in implementing robust decision-making frameworks and management systems, fostering cultures of empowerment and operational discipline, and driving continuous improvement initiatives. He is the founder of Enabling Empowerment, a consulting firm dedicated to helping organizations break the cycle of micromanagement and unlock the full potential of their teams. Chris holds a B.S. in Business Administration from Saint Louis University and an MBA from the University of Georgia.

www.ingramcontent.com/pod-product-compliance
Lightning Source LLC
Chambersburg PA
CBHW071545200326
41519CB00021BB/6623